Matchbox Toys

Matchbox Toys

A guide to selecting, collecting and enjoying new and vintage models

BRUCE AND DIANE STONEBACK

THE APPLE PRESS

A QUINTET BOOK

Published by The Apple Press
6 Blundell Street
London N7 9BH

ISBN 1-85076-441-7

This book was designed and produced by
Quintet Publishing Limited
6 Blundell Street
London N7 9BH

Creative Director: Richard Dewing
Designer: James Lawrence
Project Editor: Stefanie Foster
Editor: Patricia Seligman
Photographers: Harry Rinker Jnr, Ian Howes

Typeset in Great Britain by
Central Southern Typesetters, Eastbourne
Manufactured in Hong Kong by
Regent Publishing Services Limited
Printed in Hong Kong by
Leefung-Asco Printers Limited

DEDICATION

*To our children, Margaret and Ian, who, at the ages of
5 and 3, already know that selecting a diecast toy
means buying Matchbox.*

CONTENTS

Getting into Gear 6
The History of Matchbox

The Wheels are Rolling 26
Making Matchbox

The Most Collected Lines 36

Turning on the Ignition 58
Getting Started in Collecting

Road Maps Across Time 80
Matchbox Pocket Catalogues

Keeping the Wheels Turning 86
Accessories, Gifts, Ephemera

Lledo 104

Bibliography & Acknowledgements 110

Index 111

Getting into Gear

The History of Matchbox

I n Britain, the years following World War II were, in many respects, as bleak as those in the shattered countries over which the Allies had ultimately triumphed. Many parts of the country, especially London, were still piles of rubble – the legacy of the Luftwaffe and the V-1 and V-2 rocket bombs. Food was rationed, as were many other personal and industrial staples. Men were being "demobbed", returning to jobs they had held before the war (as the law stipulated), but for many of them the war had permanently changed the way they viewed their lives and their occupations. Children who had been evacuated from the danger-ous cities during the war were reunited with families, or sad to say, learning to get on with their lives without them.

SCHOOLBOY PACT

It was against this backdrop that two school friends named Leslie Smith and Rodney Smith (who, years earlier, had both attended the Central School in Enfield, Middlesex) would meet again, return to their pre-war jobs and follow through on a school-boy pact they had made. They had agreed as boys, simply to start a company together, somewhere and somehow, employing people to produce something.

As Matchbox insider, Ray Bush (long-time col-lector, publisher of the former *UK Matchbox* and personal friend of Leslie Smith and Jack Odell) tells the story, the two Smiths had lost touch before World War II erupted. Both enlisted in the Royal Navy, however, and that is how they found one another again. Their paths crossed quite unexpec-tedly at war's end when both Rodney and Leslie were sent to a Royal Naval base near Portsmouth to be demobilized and discharged back into civilian life. Once more, they talked about their dreams of founding an engineering firm.

But there was reality to be faced first. Before the war, Leslie Smith had been an office boy in the accounts department of JR Wilson & Co, a London confirming house that specialized in shipping items to Australia, New Zealand, and the Far East. He also attended night school to study book-keeping. Before long, the eager student moved on to the buying department where he learned about factory operations and began travelling. When he rejoined the company, he became a full buyer, making many commercial contacts and travelling extensively.

Rodney, not related to Leslie, returned to his job with a diecasting firm in North London. Occasionally, they would meet and plan for their futures. Ultimately, they decided they would pool their

talents – Leslie in sales and Rodney in diecasting – and form the company they had dreamed about. In January, 1947, Lesney Products was founded, the name combining the first syllable of Leslie and the last syllable of Rodney.

EARLY PROBLEMS

Working capital was the first problem of the two fledgling entrepreneurs. Each man left the Royal Navy with £300 in his pocket, but Rodney already had gone through some of his. Leslie Smith, believ-ing in a secure future rather than in impulsive romance, even decided to wait a year before marry-ing. Finally, the two men, with a renewed total of £600, bought their first diecasting machine from Rodney's old employer.

Of course, the next challenge they faced was finding a work place. They located a rundown pub named *The Rifleman* at Edmonton in North London, which needed repair, but was offered to them at the affordable rent of £2 a week. After surveying the possibilities, the precious machine on which they had staked their future, was pos-itioned where the bar had been.

The plan they had, according to Bush, was that Leslie would run the office while Rodney handled making components required by any industry involved in mass production. Finding work for their machine to do was absolutely critical. But orders were not easy to come by.

▲ **ABOVE**
John W (Jack) Odell and Leslie Smith, founders of Lesney Products, review their line of vehicles in the mid-sixties. Less than two decades after the company was founded, they had become multi-millionaires.

◄ LEFT
Even after nightfall, employees were hard at work at the newest of seven factories in the Lesney Products Group at Hackney, London. The plant employed more than 2200 people who, in the company's heyday, helped make more than two million Matchbox toys per week.

JACK ODELL

At the same time the Smiths were struggling to keep their new business afloat, John William Odell, known as Jack, was facing a few problems of his own. Odell, who had worked for Rodney's ex-firm, was a veteran of the British Army. During the war, his main job had been piecing together tanks. When all else failed, he would improvise something himself and, so, had plenty of engineering training in the field.

Also wanting to strike out on his own, Odell purchased some war surplus equipment including lathes, millers and grinders, and figured he would set up his business in his mother's garage. While the machinery was on its way from Bedford, the local council announced that his mother's garage could not be used for any form of industrial usage. He remembered that Rodney Smith had secured an old pub and set out to find if there was a little extra room that could be used to store his machinery.

A deal was made. The two partners at Lesney offered the use of their establishment, such as it was, if Odell would pay the rent and the cost of the electricity he used. Odell agreed, and so was born one of the most productive and creative alliances in toy-making history.

Odell set about designing his own products and as the three men worked under the same roof, Jack's skill soon became apparent. He was enlisted to make the dies for Lesney Products. Soon Jack's invaluable input was recognized and he became a full partner in the firm.

By late 1947, Lesney was getting enough work to keep eight men busy and possessed more than 30 moulds and dies. But the same cautious man who had postponed his wedding also continued to work at his old sales job until the mid 1950s, to make sure there was enough capital to keep the equipment running.

▼ BELOW
A variation of the early Lesney toy called the Aveling Barford Road Roller. The front rollers turned and the model had a hitch on the back.

Colour variations were numerous in the days after the War, because paints were in short supply. It was sometimes necessary for Lesney's paint procurers to change colours if a regular supplier ran out. But the retailers liked having assorted colours to sell. These two Cement Mixers, 1948, among the earliest of the Lesney toys, measured about 3½ in (8.7 cm) and show two of the colour variations.

Once the Caterpillar tractor (front right) was produced, the Lesney designers and engineers got extra mileage out of their work simply by adding a bulldozer blade to the basic tractor. Both the Caterpillar tractor and the Caterpillar bulldozers were created in 1948.

THE BREAKTHROUGH

The partners quickly learned that the end of the year was a slow time. One toy manufacturer asked Lesney to make a cap-gun part. The order did wonders for the firm's sagging supply of capital, and it helped to spark a creative energy as the men came to realize they also were quite capable of producing items other than industrial castings.

According to Bush, some employees also asked if they could make toys for their children during this slow time. Permission was granted, but only if it was a combined effort by everyone with toys being sold to retail shops.

By studying Dinky toys, the partners came up with a line of "economy models", that is, vehicles and one piece of heavy equipment that sold for much less than the Dinky models: a Diesel Road Roller, a Cement Mixer, a Caterpillar/Crawler Tractor, and a Caterpillar/Crawler Bulldozer, which was the tractor with a few added parts.

The Aveling Barford Diesel Road Roller, the first in the line, was not boxed. A tray holding a dozen was taken around the local shops in Tottenham, including Woolworths, to convince managers of local toy shops to sell the new toys to the public. Painted in a variety of colours and with other assorted variations, these early toys now are very hard to find.

Dinky's marketing system, limiting its wares to exclusive toy shops, and selling still other pieces directly to the public, helped Matchbox get into many new markets. Shopkeepers who hadn't been permitted to carry Dinky were thrilled to have something comparable to sell.

KOHNSTAM FAMILY

In 1947 to 1948, a new player was brought into the unfolding Lesney panorama. He was Richard Kohnstam of J. Kohnstam & Co. The Kohnstam family were already influential in British toy-making circles. Moses Kohnstam, a German, had owned and operated a toy selling business since 1875. Under the "Moko" trademark, the firm sold toys made by other, mostly German, toymakers and by 1894 had assembled a huge array of toys that were sold in most of Europe.

Established in Britain since 1890, at the outbreak of World War I the firm of M. Kohnstam & Co. was requisitioned. Son Julius, however, in 1912 had struck out on his own with a doll-making workshop in London. When the war ceased in 1918, Julius was ready to take up where he had ended with a toy business known as James Garfield & Co. In 1923, Julius also incorporated a business known as J. Kohnstam & Co, Ltd to market tin-plated clock-work toys mostly imported from Germany. Several items sold by this new company bore the old "Moko" label.

With the rise of Adolf Hitler and the increasingly hostile attitude towards Jews in Germany, Julius decided that he needed to build a firm financial base for the company which might someday be required to support other family members as well. So, in 1933, he formed the company Dollies Ltd to produce dolls in Buckinghamshire. In 1934, with the passage of the first Nuremberg laws, brother Emil joined Julius in Britain with Emil becoming the head of the new company. In addition to dolls, the company also began importing cut-priced toys from Germany, with all the profits from the sales being placed into accounts which were eventually to be used to aid other Jews escape Germany in 1937 and 1938.

Julius died in 1935, leaving brother Emil and son Richard to take care of the family's toy operations. With the outbreak of World War II in 1939 Richard went off to fight while his uncle remained to help the companies struggle through the war. With the end of the war in 1945, Richard and Emil continued the business of selling and distributing diecast toys and would make "Moko" their registered trademark in 1949.

The men didn't take long to discover the thriving newcomer to the scene: Lesney. The relationship eventually ended up with the Kohnstams' having the rights to virtually all Lesney marketing in the United Kingdom.

◄ LEFT

A general view of the Hackney Wick area of East London clearly shows the relationship of the three principal factories in the Lesney Products Group. In the lower half of the picture was the newest, ultra-modern plant at Lee Conservancy Road, alongside the Canal. In the upper half of the picture, the Eastway plants were situated just a few hundred yards from the new factory.

Lesney to keep the basic toys and the accompanying milk crates together, until they reached the toy shops.)

Neither the rag-and-bone cart nor the soapbox racer sold well, but Jack Odell always stated that the soapbox racer was the only real failure among the early Lesney toys. About 1400 were made and anyone who has one of them today is very fortunate.

▲ ABOVE

The milk float (or cart) was pulled by a single horse and came equipped with a driver and crates of milk bottles. It was the first model to be packed in its own individual box, rather than simply arriving at the retailer's shop in a large box containing 6 or 12 of the models.

▼ BELOW

This sought-after prime mover was imprinted with "British Road Services #37" on the door as well as "MAX 20 mph". Green panels on either side of the engine compartment could be removed so aspiring "young mechanics" could make "repairs". The set also included a bulldozer with "Lesney" printed on the back of the blade, and the hauling trailer with "Lesney Moko". It even came with a set of two small loading ramps so the bulldozer could be driven onto the trailer when it was time to move it.

YEARS OF GROWTH

Lesney's equipment and production schedule were running as smoothly as a finely tuned engine when it became incorporated in March 1949 as a private company producing toys and diecastings. The quarters at *The Rifleman*, ultimately to be fated to the wrecking ball, were replaced by newer facilities in the East End of London.

There were occasional bumps, however. Bush recounted, "After the move, Lesney purchased its first delivery truck, a Ford Thames van. It was painted in the then-current company livery, grey and red. The driver set off on the first delivery run from the new factory, turned onto the main road, and promptly wound up in a collision with a London bus!"

The two Smiths and Odell were eager to bring out more toys, all diecast and a bit larger than the line that would be developed and known as Matchbox Kingsize. A horse-drawn milk cart, a horse-drawn rag-and-bone cart, and a soapbox racer, headed for the streets and race tracks that children would build in their backyards.

The milk cart is significant in that it is the first of the company's early products that would come out in its own box. (Most likely, it was an attempt by

▲ ABOVE

Jumbo the Elephant, 4 in (10 cm) long and 3½ in (8.5 cm) high, **was a wind-up tin toy with diecast legs that were made by Lesney.**

The Prime Mover, Trailer and Bulldozer was issued in 1950 for a short while before the zinc embargo. This toy was the largest of the early Lesney toys and came boxed with, and bore, the "Moko" name along with Lesney's. For Moko, Jumbo the Elephant was created in 1950. The toy, with a wind-up movement, was based on a model produced earlier in Germany. Lesney found contractors to do all the work on the elephant with the exception of the diecast legs which they wanted to make. After all, they were trying to establish themselves as significant players in the British diecast toy industry.

The large and elaborate gold-coloured coach, with King and Queen riding inside, is the hardest of the variations to find. There are others containing only the Queen as well as coaches that differ in colour (gold-plated, gold-painted, or silver).

MODEL OF STATE COACH

Also, plans were set for creating a large casting of the Royal State Coach containing the figures of King George VI and his wife, Queen Elizabeth. Although at least one source maintains that a few of them were made, Jack Odell insists that none were produced.

No one could foresee the Korean War looming directly ahead. With the beginning of that conflict, zinc use in toys was banned by the Government. Although Lesney had stockpiled considerable supplies of zinc (an ingredient of the mazac metal used for the diecast toys), its use was permitted for only vital products. Because toys didn't fit into that category, Lesney again fell on somewhat harsh

times. The first casualty of the zinc ruling was the large State Coach. The substantial mould for the Coach saw other service during this period and, according to Bush, was used to prop up the leg of Jack Odell's desk.

Most of Lesney's other work had been dropped in favour of its newly created line of toys. Thinking that he foresaw the ultimate demise of Lesney, Rodney Smith decided to leave the venture. To end his involvement with Lesney, Leslie Smith and Jack Odell paid him $8000, the sum they could manage to scrape together in ready cash.

Meanwhile, Lesney, which had prudently stockpiled tons of zinc, needed something to help weather the ban on the non-essential use of the metal. Odell, through his contacts in the automobile industry, helped secure a contract for making cast-

The miniature coronation coach, like the earlier larger one, came in either gold or silver and was a Lesney Product for 1953. Its popularity, according to a pocket catalogue, triggered the Matchbox 1–75 series of miniatures. Many of these coaches were used in Britain to decorate cakes for weddings, birthdays and anniversaries.

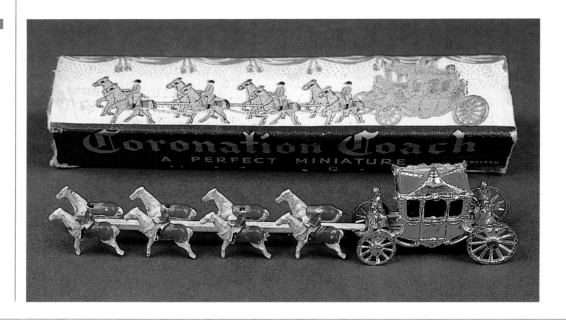

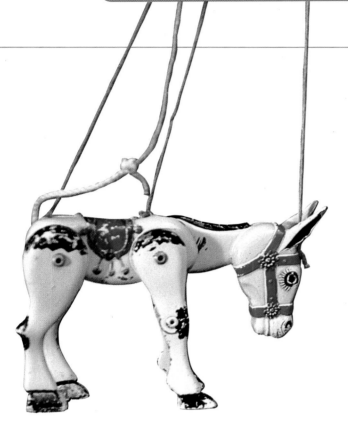

ings used in car production. More machinery was procured, and Lesney made handsome profits using the scarce and precious zinc that had been stockpiled.

With the ending of the zinc ban, and the Coronation of Queen Elizabeth II in 1953, the time was just right for the issue of the large Royal State Coach that had been started before the Korean conflict.

A problem had arisen though. The 16-in (40.5-cm) version of the coach was originally designed to show the late King and his Queen inside it. The decision was made not to modify the coach because it was assumed that Prince Philip would ride with the new Queen and having the two figures would still be appropriate. Just over one hundred of the coaches containing the two torsos were made when it was announced that Her Majesty would ride alone. Very quickly, the male figure was machined out of the mould. This change accounts for the original story, that the coach was made for the 1951 Festival of Britain. Ultimately, over 33,000 State Coaches were made and sold.

Also, with the end of the zinc ban, Lesney produced Muffin the Mule, an animal character from a popular BBC children's show, for Moko. The Lesney name did not appear anywhere on the finger marionette.

Odell then created a miniature of the Royal State Coach which would push Lesney to the forefront of the diecast toy makers who populated north-east London. Ultimately, the company would produce and market more than one million miniature Coronation Coaches. However, many of these very fragile miniatures were damaged or destroyed.

MATCHBOX IS BORN

On the heels of the small Coronation Coach came the idea for more miniatures and the use of matchboxes to hold the Lesney toys. Odell's oldest daughter could only take to school a plaything that could fit into a matchbox.

Earlier, Jack had been toying with all kinds of ideas for new and tiny toys and of these, a miniature road roller made from brass, fitted snugly in his daughter's small box. As a result, Jack Odell was swamped with requests from her schoolmates to make additional road rollers for them. This prompted Jack to make a mould to use in casting copies of his miniature toy. The initial outlay to make it was about £100 and enabled him to make as many copies of the toy as he needed.

The potential in this great, untapped market for miniature toys was mind-boggling. Dinky toys, after all, were much larger in comparison. While the other partners were contemplating just what Jack's brainstorm could mean to the company, he was discovering a matchbox from the Norvic Match Co Ltd of Czechoslovakia which contained the new toy perfectly. Matchbox had been created.

Appearing in 1951, Muffin the Mule was a small puppet manipulated by four strings. Based on a popular television character in the early 1950s, Muffin had a string tail. His box was marked "MOKO" and "Made in England".

The Norvic Matchbox was to provide the inspiration for Matchbox toys, and the similarities are obvious, even down to the indented border-line and the rendering of the sky in the background.

1–75 SERIES

The Aveling Barford Road Roller (No 1), the Muir Hill Site Dumper (No 2), the Cement Mixer (No 3) and the Massey Harris Tractor (No 4), all scaled down from the earlier and larger Christmas toys, were the first miniatures in the new 1–75 series.

Made in 1953, they were packaged in yellow and blue small boxes and bore the lines "Matchbox' Series" and "A Moko Lesney Product" with the name "Moko" in italic script. (For subsequent issues of the models, new boxes that put the name "Moko" into block letters, were created.) In addition, the number of the issued toy was printed on each box. The men waited for the reaction.

After a slow start, the New Year brought good fortune to the company. Sales started picking up, particularly after the introduction of the London double-decker bus (No 5). One of the theories was that children liked being able to buy a whole toy so cheaply. Wholesalers began clamouring for more of this new line from Lesney. Soon, new issues followed: the Quarry Truck (No 6), the Horse-drawn Milk Float (No 7), the Caterpillar Tractor (No 8), and the Dennis Fire Engine (No 9).

These toys became so popular that Lesney Products had to expand and, although industrial diecasting remained a very big item for the company, the production of toys became an ever-increasing interest. Lesney's were still a small firm during their initial period, employing only two or three people and with limited resources. They had no warehouses for storage. Leslie Smith was still working for Wilson's at the time.

Problems arose for Leslie and Jack when they discovered that Richard Kohnstam had already registered the trademark "Matchbox" based upon his recollections of having packaged tiny wooden dolls in matchboxes during his youth. Unhappy about this turn of events, and in preparation for the eventual breakup of this alliance, Leslie Smith and Odell decided that the name "Moko" would not appear on any of the toys themselves. But for the moment, Kohnstam was entitled to market the hot new toys at home and in Europe, as well as a few other locations.

So Smith, who, from his previous sales job had important contacts throughout the world, turned his attention to other markets where Moko was not in the way, particularly the United States, New Zealand and Australia.

◄ LEFT
The Massey Harris Tractor, an early Lesney toy, towers over the miniature that was modelled after it. The miniature was only 1½ in (3.7 cm) long.

► RIGHT
The Aveling Barford Road Roller No 1 was the first vehicle in the Matchbox 1–75 series of miniatures. Like the earlier Lesney toy, the miniature's front roller turned and it had a rear hitch. New was the addition of a driver.

▲ **ABOVE**

The second miniature in the line was the Muir Hill Site Dumper, also manned by a driver. The ride must have been a rough one as the model moved on metal wheels.

▼ **BELOW**

A red, double-decker bus that appeared in 1954, was a great seller. It said "No. 5" on the front and back, had a flashy gold radiator and encouraged all who saw it to "Buy 'Matchbox' Series".

▲ **ABOVE**

The quarry truck No 6 picked up the company's construction theme again. This one had an orange cab, grey dumper, grey wheels and gold radiator.

▲ **TOP**

A cement mixer was the third model in the line that was heavily into construction vehicles. There were various colour combinations – blue with orange wheels and blue with grey metal wheels.

Numbering Systems

It won't take the Matchbox novice collector long to discover the often-bewildering world of the Matchbox numbering system.

Up until 1982, and the takeover by Universal, the numbered identification system was fairly straightforward. Within the 1–75 miniature series, every time a new model was brought out, it was assigned a number, from 1 to 75, and a letter to indicate its place in the models of that number since the inception of the Matchbox range. For example, in the model line-up of number 20 in the regular wheels series, 20A is an ERF Heavy Lorry; 20B is an ERF 686 Truck; 20C is a Chevrolet Taxi; 20D is a Lamborghini Marzal; 20E is a Police Patrol Car; 20F is a 4×4 Jeep with roof; 20G is a Volvo Container Truck; and 20H is a Volkswagen Transporter. As this list shows, there is no pattern in such issues and industrial offerings are mixed in with both exclusive and mundane marques of cars. Models 76 and 77 were issued during the crisis year 1980.

Within various numbers and letters, however, models often were changed. These changes were in body colour, plastic windows were added, deleted, or changed in colour and occasionally, wheel colours were altered. Models that were so changed could be introduced as a new model and assigned a new letter within the model's number; sometimes, the re-coloured model was even given a new number along with a new letter. More often, however, the number and letter of the offering were kept the same with the change being listed as a "variation".

▶ RIGHT

A gold set of 1–75s re-issues. Very few of these sets were produced in gold plate as opposed to paint. They were given to senior staff at Matchbox in celebration of forty years of Matchbox production.

◀ LEFT

This reversed colour Wreck Truck was initially produced in tiny quantities with the company colours incorrectly applied. As you can see from the box illustration, they should have been the other way round!

"NUMBER-LETTER-NUMBER" SYSTEM

Collectors needed a way to identify a model's place within the line-up and also its colour and other variations. Though "unofficial", that need resulted in a "number-letter-number" system whereby the number and letter were determined by the range and its sequence within that range and the various colour differences were noted by including a number after the letter – one number for each known colour variation. For example, in the 22B model (a 1958 Vauxhall Cresta), 22B1 has a pinkish-cream body, no plastic windows, and grey plastic wheels. Model 22B2, the same colour and also windowless, has grey plastic wheels. 22B3 is the same pinkish-cream colour, but it has green plastic windows and grey plastic wheels. Up to variation No 6, the models have a very slight colour change and remove or add windows. Then, with 22B7, the colour changes to gun-metal grey; 22B8, to dull bronze; 22B9, to bright bronze, and 22B10, to grey and pink, and so on.

DISINTEGRATION OF THE NUMBERING SYSTEM

Beginning in 1981, any stability within the numbering system was blown to pieces. In that year, the system was changed to produce different lines for the United States and the rest of the world (ROW). Some models – the "core" line-up – were common to both the US and the ROW and even used the same number but, to confuse matters, a few appear in both series but use different numbers. Further confusion arises as various models appear in one range but not in the other and, occasionally, a model that would prove popular in the one range would suddenly be issued in the other range under the same or a different number. Add to that a separate line with completely different numbers for Japan and you are left with one giant headache for the collector.

As a result, in 1982, the model numbers disappeared from the undersides of the vehicles because, with the two different lines, putting numbers on them was leading to problems even for Matchbox itself.

MODELS OF YESTERYEAR NUMBERING

The Models of Yesteryear range is numbered a bit differently. Each model is given a number but then numbers are also used to designate the position the model holds within that number. For example, Y1-1 is the Allchin Traction Engine issued in 1956; Y1-2, a 1911 Model T Ford (1964); and Y1-3, a 1936 SS100 Jaguar (1977). Issues of a current model in new liveries do not result in a renumbering of any sort. Occasionally, one might see the Yesteryears line listed in a "number-letter" system whereby a Y-1A would be equivalent to a Y1-1. (Beginning with the 1988 catalogue, Matchbox changed the "Y" Yesteryears prefix to "YY".)

SKYBUSTERS

Skybusters generally are numbered according to the type of aircraft. An SB10 is a Boeing 747. Changes in livery are not recorded as new models. However, a few models have changed within numbered line-ups; for instance, the SB3, an A300 Airbus, was withdrawn and replaced with the US NASA Space Shuttle and the SB12, a Skyhawk A4F, was replaced with the Pitts Special. These two new models within those two numbered series are SB3.2 and SB12.2 respectively.

Occasionally, when two liveries are available concurrently for the same model, the distinctions are differentiated with a letter added to the number. The SB23, a Concorde, is available in both the British Airways livery (SB23A) and the Air France livery (SB23B).

▲ ABOVE

This Skybusters shop display unit is surmounted by a sketch of the NASA

Space Shuttle – a model that was introduced in 1979 as an SB3.

▶ RIGHT

This early Lesney Milk Float in blue is far rarer than the orange version. It may even have been a promotional model for a local dairy company as all the collected examples have been found in Britain.

▼ BELOW

The popularity of the horse-drawn milk float as an early Lesney toy led it to be recreated in miniature. It earned its special place in Matchbox history as the only horse-drawn issue in the entire line of 1–75 diecast miniatures.

OPENING UP THE MARKET

At first, there were several importers recruited for the United States Matchbox market, but the Fred Bronner Corporation became the sole importer in 1956. The Models of Yesteryear series was unveiled in 1956 and was based on another of Jack Odell's brainstorms. The skilled engineer who designed all the machinery for Lesney models, wanted to make more detailed models as well as feature antique trucks, buses, and fire engines that he really liked. Although Leslie Smith had originally opposed the new line (especially the word "yesteryear", which Smith pointed out could not be found in any then-current dictionary), the success of the idea has a 36-year history.

▼ BELOW
Early Models of Yesteryear display stand. Matchbox were pioneers in the field of "point of sale" material, and items such as this very early unit were always made of card. As a result they are very hard to come by, but are very collectable, as they still provide a most attractive way of displaying a collection.

No 1	Allchin Steam Engine	59¢	No 4	Steam Lorry	59¢	No 7	4 Ton Leyland Truck	59¢
No 2	Double Decker Bus	59¢	No 5	Le Mans Bentley 1929	59¢	No 8	1926 Morris Cowley	59¢
No 3	Double Decker Tram Car	59¢	No 6	World War I Lorry	59¢	No 9	Showman's Engine	98¢

▼ BELOW

One of the early Models of Yesteryear gift sets, G-7, was assembled in 1961 and included: the Y-3 1907 London E Class Tram Car that contained a "News of the World" advertisement on the top as well as "Buy Lesney Toys" and markings for the London Transport System; the Y-8 Morris Cowley 1926 Bullnose; the Y-9 Fowler Showman's Engine with "Lesney's Modern Amusements" printed along the roofline; the Y-12 London Horse-drawn Bus with "Lipton's Tea" in decals on the top deck; and the Y-14 Duke of Connaught Engine from the Great Western Railway.

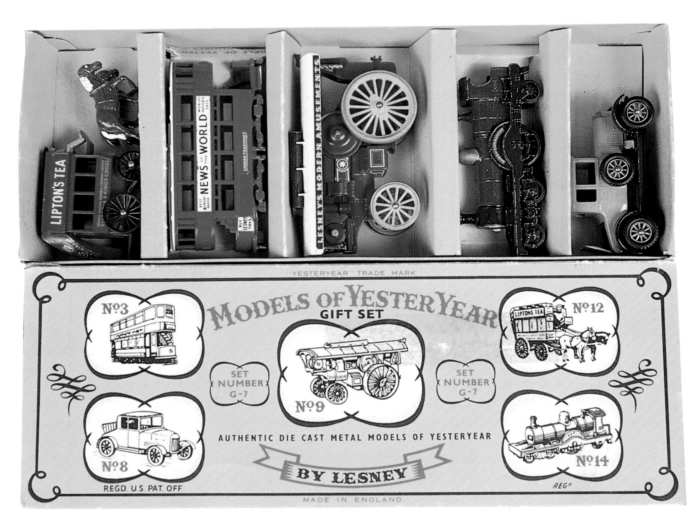

► RIGHT

This limited edition No 04692 framed Models of Yesteryear presentation featured the Leyland Titan TD1 bus. It contained a painting of how the vehicle looked as it transported people through British towns, a fully assembled vehicle, and then a breakdown-style display of all the parts that were used to assemble the bus. This version advertised "Swan Fount Pens" and the entire presentation measured 21 by 13 in (52.5 by 32.5 cm).

BATTLE WITH KOHNSTAM

In 1956 the showdown came with Richard Kohnstam over the registration of the name "Matchbox". In what appears to have been a somewhat acrimonious confrontation, Leslie Smith threatened to remove the names "Matchbox" and "Moko" from all connections with the toys simply by throwing away the boxes. Kohnstam, who realized that only by compromise might he retain his lucrative association, agreed to re-register the name "Matchbox" to Lesney and Moko. From that point on, however,

Lesney waited for the chance to force out Kohnstam. Lesney soon won a small skirmish in the war when Richard Kohnstam was not given a role in the sale of the newly-created Models of Yesteryear.

After complaints about Kohnstam's handling of some export markets, Lesney bought out Richard Kohnstam in 1958, and the name Moko was immediately phased out of all Lesney packaging. Shortly thereafter Lesney would also buy out Fred Bronner's US operations, making it a wholly owned subsidiary of the parent company. Bronner, however, remained in charge of the American subsidiary.

▲ ABOVE
The first vehicle in the Major Pack series was the Caterpillar DW20 Earth Scraper. It was to be one of 15 vehicles in the line. The underside of the tractor was marked "Made in England No. 1 by Lesney" and the sides were marked with "CAT DW20". This line of Major Pack vehicles was the forerunner of the King and SuperKing range.

▼ BELOW
This magnificent model of Pickford's Low Loader Major Pack was easily the largest of the Major Pack series. This later example is finished in brighter and lighter colours than the original but it is this one that is hard to find.

THE GOOD YEARS

The decision to sell shares and go public was not made by the owners of Lesney, but by their accountants. British tax laws required the public ownership of at least 25 per cent of the company if the firm were to avoid payment of a confiscatory surtax. Some 400,000 25 pence shares of company stock were offered to the public at £1 each. There were plenty of investors as offers to purchase the stock ran up to more than six million shares.

Also in 1960, Peter Webb was lured away from Lesney's advertising and marketing agents to join the company. Webb, a well-known model train enthusiast, began to trumpet the virtues of Matchbox to fellow enthusiasts while pushing the company to bring out more models very close to OO in scale.

Success came quickly for Lesney: there was the Queen's Award to Industry in 1966. By that time, Lesney employed 3600 workers and was producing, according to that year's pocket catalogue, more than 100 million models annually. That same year, Fred Bronner founded an American Collectors' Club which would grow to 50,000 members in just six years.

During 1967 and 1968, the firm had sales of over £28 million with a profit so high, £5 million, that the achievement gained Lesney a special mention in the Guinness Book of World Records. Second and third Queen's Awards followed, with the OBE for Smith and Odell. Some 130 different countries were on the Matchbox road, forming eager markets for the 5.5 million models pouring from the plant each week. The future looked ever more bright.

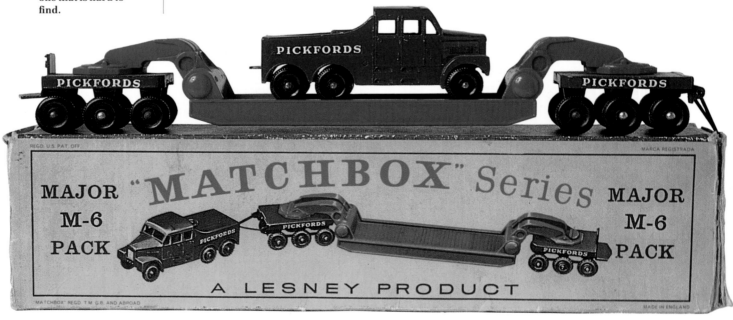

AMBUSH BY HOT WHEELS

Then, disaster struck. Mattel, Inc, an American toy producer, introduced its Hot Wheels and pounded the toy into the public's consciousness with a money's-no-object promotional campaign which reportedly cost about $10 million. Every time a television was turned on, as Odell observed during a trip to the United States, the screen was plastered with Hot Wheels commercials. The frictionless wheels and axles of this line outpaced the British toymakers.

Reluctantly, Odell ordered Research and Development into finding a system to compete with the Hot Wheels system. On one hand, Lesney was helped along by the fact that Hot Wheels production couldn't even begin to cope with early demand, but, on the other hand, Hot Wheels production was based in Hong Kong, with much lower manufacturing costs. Therefore, in addition to coming up with a new design, it was time for Lesney officials to find a way to make their cars more cheaply. The answer, they concluded, was developing more automated equipment. Meanwhile, US sales were deflating like a tyre pierced by a nail, dropping to $6 million from $28 million. The same firm that was awash in cash two years before now was out seeking loans to ensure the survival of the company. Lesney's own bank refused to lend the necessary cash but, in the end, the necessary funds were secured.

LESNEY DIVERSIFIES

The result of the crisis was the Superfast series, which became an instant hit in the UK. By 1971, most of the line had been converted to Superfast, but the firm still lost money because of the startup costs. However, the company still launched some new products, making it a time for diversification.

Plastic kits came out in 1971. To build the image of its Superfast line-up, Lesney produced the Matchbox Collectors' Club and began financing a professional racing team in Formula Two competition. The team's progress was even reported in some of the company's pocket catalogues.

One gets the impression that Lesney designers were really "on a roll". Cascade, a mechanical game, was created. In 1973, the Rola-matics were announced. These miniatures had working features that functioned as the car was pushed along. The Fighting Furies – romantic action figures like Captain Hook – were announced in 1975, and the line even included a vinyl carrying case that transformed into a Spanish galleon.

In 1978, Lesney bought AMT, an American maker of plastic model kits, and the American firm Vogue Dolls. But instead of saving the situation, these acquisitions triggered a downturn from which Lesney would not recover. As the world economy – and particularly Britain's – slipped into recession, the situation at Lesney looked grim.

▲ **ABOVE**

The Matchbox Accessory Pack No 2 was a car transporter that, like many other Lesney products, came in different colours. The all-blue model on the right, with the decal "Matchbox Car Transporter" is easier to find than the red truck and grey transporter on the left that carries the decals "Car Collection LTD". Both are marked "Matchbox Car Transporter, Accessory Pack # 2" and "Made in England by Lesney".

STRUGGLE TO SAVE
THE COMPANY

Jack Odell, who had retired in 1973, was called out of retirement by the firm's bankers, but even he was unable to stem the tide. Comparing his job to being captain of the *Titanic*, he told everyone he would stay on for just one year.

In 1980, David CW Yeh of the Universal Group, who eventually would buy the company, put down Lesney's troubles to high labour costs in the UK and the failure by the company to pay enough attention to the American market by producing American cars for American kids.

He suggested that Lesney try switching some production from the UK to Asia. Leslie Smith balked, not wanting to give away technological secrets. Yeh pointed out that Asian production techniques were already superior to those being used at Lesney.

Lesney challenged Universal to produce two models that had been abandoned in England because of high production costs. They were numbered 76 and 77 to mute criticism of this action within the UK. Both models were finished when expected and came in at the specified cost.

WINDING UP LESNEY

In June 1982, the end came. Receivers were appointed and, as required by British law, the name Lesney disappeared from the list of actively trading companies. In Lesney's place, a company called Matchbox Toys was created to serve as a holding company for all of the former Lesney operations. Yeh, who was thoroughly familiar with the company's problems but still wanted to buy it, flew to London and made an offer. He won the prize after several other bidders dropped out. On 24 September 1982 David Yeh became the head of Universal Matchbox.

Hastily assembled assortments of Matchbox miniatures were packed under the "Dinky" label soon after Universal Matchbox purchased the long-time Matchbox competitor. The effort was intended to protect the trademark until engineers and designers actually determined the direction Universal would take with Dinky.

Matchbox follow the success of their Thunderbirds range with the launch of Stingray in 1993. This range of toys has never before been produced in diecast metal, despite the original TV series being made nearly 30 years ago.

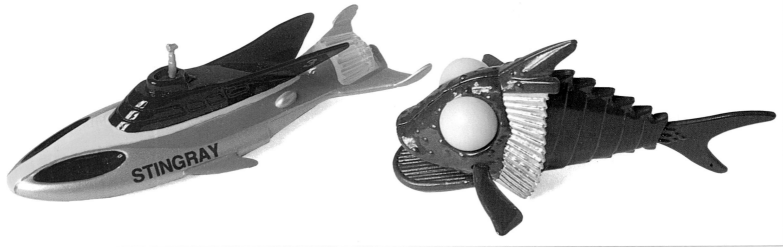

UNIVERSAL MATCHBOX

Universal already did most of its own manufacturing in Macau, and production of Matchbox miniatures was moved there from England. Research and Design headquarters, however, remained in the UK, as did production of the Models of Yesteryear (until 1987) and the plastic model kits. By the end of 1987, all Matchbox diecast vehicles had been moved to Macau or to a new factory opened in the People's Republic of China.

In 1987, Universal Matchbox bought the Dinky trademark and made plans to expand its diecast vehicle range further while quickly packaging a number of Matchbox miniatures under the Dinky trademark simply to keep it protected.

On 13 July 1992, after a number of on-again, off-again negotiations, Tyco Toys Inc, an American toy company and the fourth largest of the world's toymakers, announced that it had agreed to purchase Universal Matchbox Group Ltd for $106 million in cash and stocks.

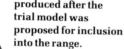

▲ ABOVE

The "My First Matchbox" range was a great success when it was launched in 1991. This example was not produced after the trial model was proposed for inclusion into the range.

THE FUTURE OF MATCHBOX

What does the future hold for Matchbox under the auspices of Tyco Toys Inc? Unfortunately, not much is known about Tyco's plans for Matchbox yet the reasons for Tyco's acquisitions of Universal Matchbox hint at its future course. Before acquiring Matchbox, Tyco's sales were concentrated in the US with only 14 per cent overseas. What Universal Matchbox has brought to Tyco is a strong international sales network.

How will this affect the Matchbox collector? Most important, the future of Matchbox as part of the Tyco empire, with sales of over $715 million, is assured. Matchbox products complement the Tyco range rather than compete with them so will not be phased out on that score. However, Tyco have announced their intention to look at cutting the high distribution and administrative costs for Matchbox.

For American collectors, Matchbox's new owners raise hopes that the North American Matchbox market (both the US and Canada) will finally receive the attention it deserves, bringing more specifically American models and the overhaul of a patchy distribution and marketing system.

But, perhaps the most fundamental change collectors hope to see is a more positive attitude by the owners of Matchbox towards the collectors of their products. After all, collecting Matchbox can only add to the strength of an already venerable toy line that, for some people, is an important part of their past, present and future.

LLEDO – THE LAST LAUGH

But the Lesney story doesn't end with receivership, Matchbox Toys, David Yeh, Universal Matchbox, or with the sale to Tyco. Jack Odell, the retired partner and the spiritual force behind Lesney for many years, decided in 1982 to begin a new company to produce a line of diecast toys within the UK. The Models of Yesteryear had been his brainchild and first love, and he decided to have his new company – Lledo – make a similar line. But Lledo and Odell's rebirth will be discussed in more detail in Chapter 7.

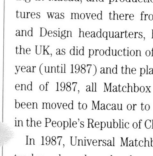

◄ LEFT

The hottest sellers in 1992 were the new Thunderbirds' models from Matchbox. The models illustrated **here are in fact the original modelmakers prototypes from which the moulds were eventually produced.**

The Wheels Are Rolling

Making Matchbox

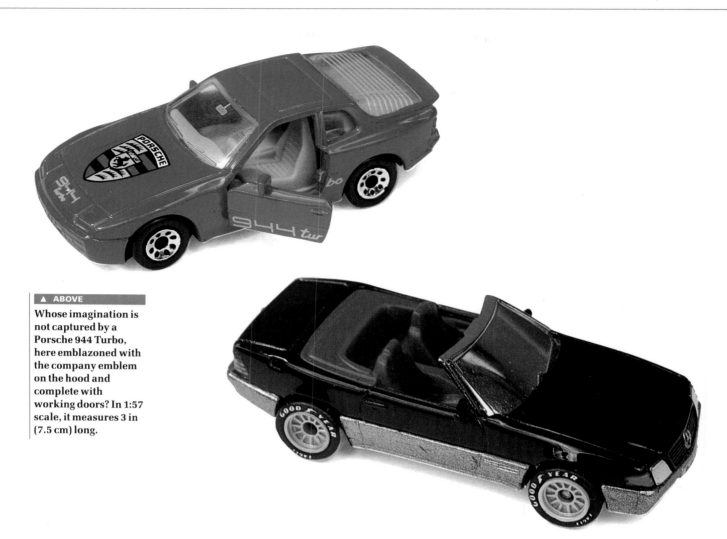

▲ ABOVE

Whose imagination is not captured by a Porsche 944 Turbo, here emblazoned with the company emblem on the hood and complete with working doors? In 1:57 scale, it measures 3 in (7.5 cm) long.

Ferraris, Jaguars, Mercedes Benzes and BMWs are expensive cars that require buyers with a healthy bank account. But adding the latest models of these internationally known vehicles to the Matchbox diecast range represents even more of an investment than simply buying a full-sized vehicle from a car showroom.

Expenses for new-model development run to millions of pounds or dollars, so that is why care is taken in selecting new cars and trucks for future Matchbox toys. They must weigh a vehicle's potential popularity against the costs to take it from the drawing board to the end of the assembly line – a process which takes nearly a year.

NEW IDEAS
FOR MATCHBOX TOYS

How does a vehicle even get considered for a Matchbox run? Members of the company's research and design department scan car magazines and visit car shows to see the latest vehicles which lead to suggestions for possible models that are considered by the Matchbox marketing directors of the United Kingdom, Germany, the United States and Australia.

According to Paul Carr, 16-year veteran of the Matchbox Research and Design Department, collectors and members of the public also send suggestions to the company.

Each marketing manager generally requests four or five models his division wants made into miniatures, but when the total of new miniatures for the year was to be about ten, compromise has been necessary. It is not difficult to see why the Germans usually want BMWs, Mercedes and Volkswagens; the Americans are interested in the latest sports or muscle cars; the Australians, on the other hand, with vehicles of all nationalities on their streets, are less demanding.

Rather than run-of-the-mill cars, the company has been more interested in selecting cars known the world over, such as BMWs and Ferraris. They have also selected cars that capture the imagination, like the super-fast Jaguar XJ220, billed as a car for millionaire motorists.

Final decisions generally favour the desires of managers from the countries with the highest Matchbox diecast sales. Recently, the United Kingdom and Germany have had the most clout, while the United States has had to take something of a back seat with only about 25 per cent of sales.

▲ ABOVE

The Mercedes 500 SL is one of the vehicles in the Matchbox line-up of World Class Wheels billed as "The Elite of Matchbox Vehicles" and "Collectors' Limited Editions". They are highly detailed and come with authentic rubber tyres. This model has mirrored windows and impressive detailing, right down to "Good Year" printed on the black rubber tyres.

RESEARCH AND DESIGN

Once compromises are made and new models are selected, the research and design department goes into action.

A widely printed Lesney Products and Co photograph taken in the mid-1960s showed chief Matchbox model designer Fred Rix and model maker Ken Wetton studying and photographing a 1907 Rolls-Royce Silver Ghost at the Measham Motor Museum in Burton-on-Trent, England, for a Models of Yesteryear replica. The process, today, for making a model is much the same.

The real vehicle must be found, whether that quest takes Matchbox representatives to a new car factory for a look at a new model before it has been released, or to a new car showroom. Studying the details generally takes two men a day to photograph the car from every angle.

Next, a rough sketch of the car itself is made for logging measurements for even when a manufacturer provides drawings of the car, they are not as accurate as they need to be.

With this information a draughtsman can make additional, very detailed, drawings three times the size of the toy – a 3-week process.

▲ ABOVE

In the days of Lesney Products, the details of a 1907 Rolls-Royce "Silver Ghost" at the Measham Motor Museum, near Burton-on-Trent, were carefully reviewed by the then chief Matchbox model designer Fred Rix (right) and modelmaker Ken Wetton for a Models of Yesteryear replica.

▶ RIGHT

A general view of the drawing office at the Matchbox Model factory at Hackney, London. This important department was responsible for all design and development in the production of Matchbox models.

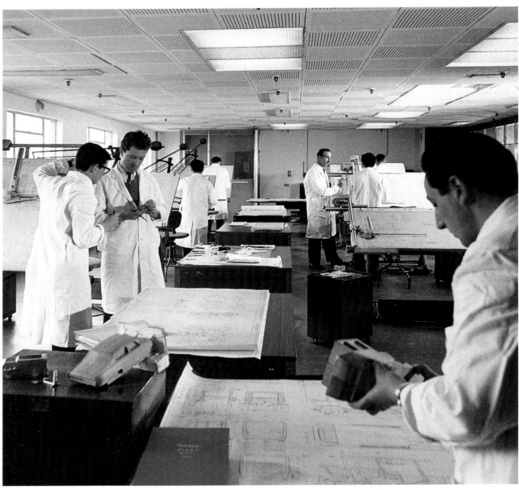

◄ LEFT

This photograph illustrates the three main stages of the development of a Matchbox model. In the background is a wooden rendition of the proposed subject, three times its eventual finished size. In the foreground is the original mock-up rendition of the model. In the middle are the unpainted, first trial castings produced to highlight faults before full production starts.

◄ LEFT
▼ BELOW

Craftsmen pattern-makers carved by hand detailed wooden patterns for new models. Resin models made from these patterns were used as guides for cutting the steel for the tools at the Hackney factory of Lesney Products.

Completed copies of their drawings are taken to two types of model makers – one who will machine and carve a model out of solid Perspex in the actual size of the toy and another who will make a wooden master model, or pattern, at three times the size of the completed toy. (The completed Perspex model often is the one photographed for use in the catalogue because it is ready long before the completed models have been produced.)

▼ BELOW

A resin model of a Mercury Sable, left, is parked next to the manufactured version that was produced and marketed by Matchbox. The 3-in (7.5-cm) long finished model was 1:63 in scale and was labelled "Made in Macau, Matchbox Intl. Ltd".

MANUFACTURING THE MODELS

A 1980 Matchbox Collectors' Club Official Handbook provides the information for what happened next in the days when the models were still being made in Britain. First moulds, carved from a special chrome-vanadium steel, were put into an automatic diecasting machine from which over one million models were cast. On the assembly line the castings were automatically ejected from the moulds falling onto a conveyor belt. The rough castings were then tumbled and deburred, removing all excess metal and creating a smooth surface. Next, the models had all grease, acid and dirt removed, so that the models could be painted.

In those days, the paint shop sprayed more than 2000 gallons of lead-free paint on the castings that were headed to buyers around the world. While the paint shop applied colourful finishes to more than 8 million parts daily, the plastic shop used 60 large plastic moulding machines to produce miniature wheels, seats, tyres and other parts by the million.

Once metal and plastic parts were ready, they were put together on 20 different assembly lines. On each side of the lines, technicians used automatic machines to install windows and other plastic parts and fasten the model to the base plate. By the late 1970s, decals were applied automatically, where women had once had to apply the decals and paint detailing by hand.

◄ LEFT
One of Lesney's 160 tool makers in the six tool rooms at the Hackney factory, checked the final details on one of the two-impression high-speed diecast moulds.

► RIGHT
In the mid-sixties, the company used 17 paint-spraying machines which gave each miniature a complete coating of lead-free paint which was then baked on for maximum strength and a quality finish.

▲ ABOVE
View of one of the three huge foundries at the Matchbox factory where Lesney had 130 machines producing diecastings for models. Designed and constructed by Lesney engineers, each of the fully automatic machines had a daily output that could exceed 10,000 car bodies.

Once assembled, packaging machines formed and shaped the boxes and then the new models were inserted and shipped around the world. "If the models from a year's work in these factories were placed front to back, they would stretch from London to San Francisco, a distance of more than 5000 miles."

In more recent days, however, copies of the draughtsmen's drawings, photographs, master patterns and the Perspex models have been forwarded to the Hong Kong headquarters of Universal Matchbox before being sent to various production facilities in the Far East.

Simplifying a complicated process, resin castings are made of component parts of the model, three times the completed vehicle size, which are then copied down to the size of the model on machines called "pantographs". In use even during Lesney days, a pantograph cuts the delicate outline of a new Matchbox series model in high quality chrome steel, using a tiny needle in its cutter that is as fine as many a modern dentists' high speed drill. The steel portion of the mould is then hand-fitted and rough castings are taken to check that the mould-making has been accurate. Finally, tool makers check details on high speed diecast moulds used in the foundries that produce the diecastings that become the painted, finished models.

▲ TOP LEFT
Spray-painting machines could coat thousands of model cars per hour. Here, caravan trailer bodies are being coated as they travel on a moving belt, en route to the oven.

▲ TOP RIGHT
Women, in one of the main assembly shops at the Lesney factory, carried out the final steps in assembling components and giving life to the models. During Lesney's good years, more than 2000 women manned the assembly lines.

▲ ABOVE
It took nimble fingers to add tiny decals and transfers to the models in the days before the tampo printing process had been developed.

A Selection of Unusual Collectible Models

This gold plated Leyland Tiger fire engine can normally only be found with silver-plated detailing. The brass-effect version was considered too garish for general consumption.

LONDON AIRPORT AUTHORITY

6

This enormous Fire Engine was abandoned after only 50 models had been completed. It was to have featured a working pump and lights, but was considered too expensive to manufacture.

Prototype models are nearly always different from the finished products. This mock-up prototype Y7 Breakdown Truck has a much larger tow hook than the first version, as well as a roof made from parts of other models.

Very few of the Y9–1 Showman's Engines were produced with this strange purple effect. Normally the body colour of this model varied from deep maroon to bright red.

▲ ABOVE

This is a prototype of the Scorpion powered car which carried no batteries but whose engine could be activated by a power charger. These models are now rare and serve, perhaps, as a reflection of how concerned Lesney was by the competition from Mattel.

▲ ABOVE

The Number 49 Unimog was not originally intended to be sold to the public. It was used as a trial model for apprentice engineers to practise on. It was in development for two years before finally being released.

► RIGHT

The Y16–1 Spyker was a very popular model, but is normally only found in either light or dark yellow. No-one really knows why this maroon version came into being, but it is very desirable to many collectors.

Colour Variations

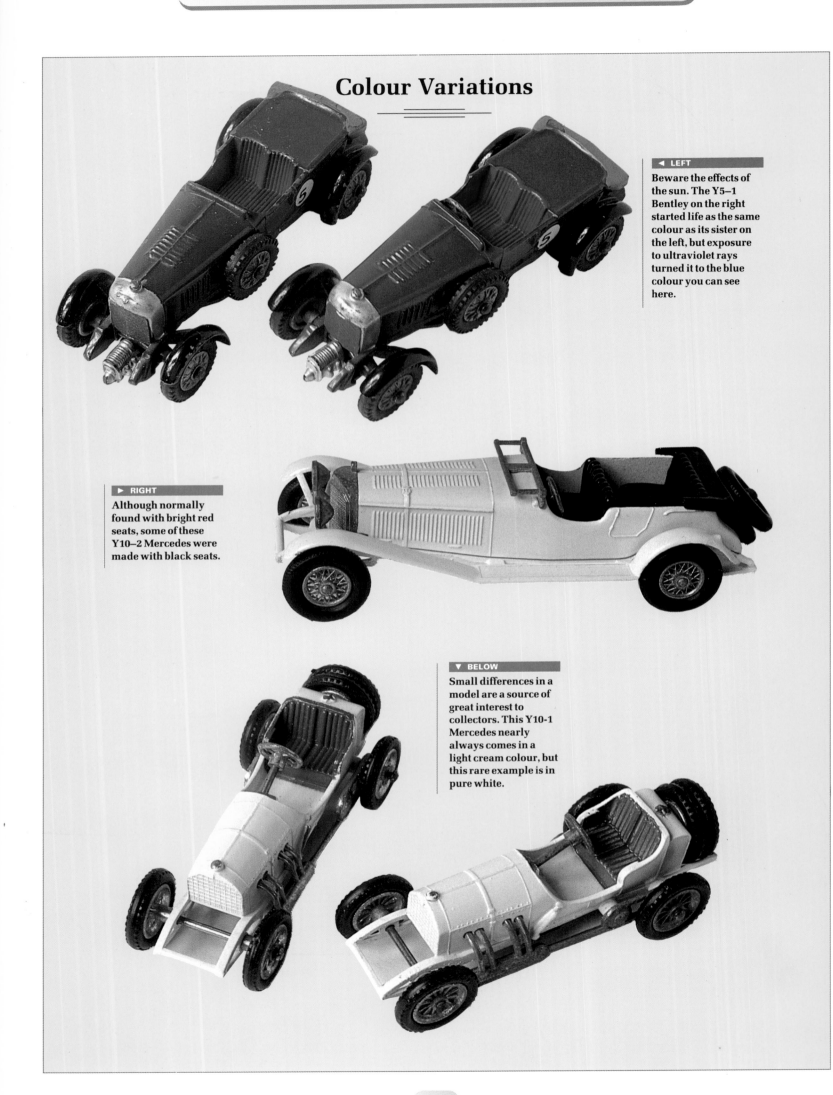

◄ LEFT
Beware the effects of the sun. The Y5–1 Bentley on the right started life as the same colour as its sister on the left, but exposure to ultraviolet rays turned it to the blue colour you can see here.

► RIGHT
Although normally found with bright red seats, some of these Y10–2 Mercedes were made with black seats.

▼ BELOW
Small differences in a model are a source of great interest to collectors. This Y10-1 Mercedes nearly always comes in a light cream colour, but this rare example is in pure white.

MATCHBOX QUALITY

The quality and detail of Matchbox models has been recognized by collectors from all over the world. The same attention to detail, however, apparently has earned Matchbox even greater honours. According to the 1980 collectors' handbook, representatives of the Smithsonian Institution selected an assortment of Matchbox models to represent their real, full-sized counterparts and included them in time capsules as part of the Helium Centennial, 1868–1968.

These capsules will be opened in 1993, 2018, 2068 and 2968. The handbook commentary concludes: "Just as your collection will help you to grow with the times, these time-capsule Matchbox collections will tell future generations about today's cars and vehicles."

◄ LEFT
Electronics and automation were vital in the 200,000 square foot Hackney plant where the entire factory was interconnected by mechanized remote-controlled handling. In the end, however, the system wasn't efficient enough to compete with cheaper labour and more advanced technology in the Far East.

The Most Collected Lines

▲ ABOVE
The Massey Harris Tractor 745 D had "Made in England" stamped inside one fender and "A Lesney Product" inside the other. According to one collector, the red tractors shipped to the United States had screws holding on the big rear tyres while those marketed in England had painted-over nails. The rear tyres were put on backwards at the factory so that the tread went the wrong way.

While any of the Matchbox ranges offer the first-time collector enough options to begin his or her journey through the world of Matchbox, there are certain popular models of Matchbox production, both current and past, which consistently find their way into the major collections.

There even seem to be national preferences, with collectors in one country seeking out models avoided by most collectors from other countries. This obviously affects the prices that these models command in their respective countries.

EARLY LESNEY TOYS

Prior to 1953 and the introduction of the first die-cast miniature, Lesney began making toys as a sideline to its other business of manufacturing die-cast items for a wide range of British industry. For the most part, the early items were not packaged in individual boxes but, instead, were shipped in large boxes containing a dozen of each toy in a rainbow of colours. The individual boxing of the models began officially in 1949 with the production of the Horse-drawn Milk Cart, sometimes referred to as a "float".

Produced during this period, from 1948 to 1955, were the Aveling Barford Road Roller, Cement Mixer, Crawler Tractor (sometimes called a Cater-

pillar Tractor), Crawler Bulldozer (Caterpillar Bulldozer), the Horse-drawn Milk Cart, the Rag-and-bone Cart, the Soapbox Racer, Jumbo the Elephant, the Prime Mover, Trailer and Bulldozer (a heavy-duty pulling engine, a trailer, and a bulldozer that were packaged as a set), Muffin the Mule, Large Coronation Coach, Small Coronation Coach, Massey-Harris Tractor, the Bread Bait Press (a device that compressed bread for use as fishing bait inspired by Jack Odell's love of fishing), and a Covered Wagon.

Several models that were conceived but never released later formed the bases for some of the early miniature models and at least one was turned into a Models of Yesteryear issue.

A number of the early toys were marketed with accessories. The Milk Cart came with a driver with his arms outstretched and six metal milk crates filled with bottles; the Rag-and-bone Cart came with a similar driver and an assortment of diecast "junk" to add realism.

Colours varied, because as Jack Odell pointed out, in the years after the War, and even into the early 1950s virtually everything was rationed and shortages in industrial materials were particularly bad. Paint was in tight supply and, sometimes, to keep the lines running, models were painted in whatever colour Lesney could find. This also accounts for differing shades of the same colour because the paints were coming from any supplier who happened to have some to sell.

Some rare specimens include any model of the Rag-and-bone Cart (green ones are especially rare) and the Soapbox Racer. Blue milk floats are also rare and highly prized by collectors who have them.

▼ BELOW
It is thought that the Soap Box Racer shown here may never have actually gone on sale as only ten complete examples are known to exist worldwide. This one is on display at the Chester Toy Museum.

MB38s

Matchbox has had more mileage out of its Model A Ford Van (38G) than any other vehicle it has ever produced. That is because the van has been marketed not only as a regular issue in the 1–75 line of miniatures but also as a promotional model.

Matchbox made promotional models for many other companies and attractions. But this particular MB38 was made to promote Matchbox itself and was distributed at the New York Toy Fair in 1984. The event was marked on the roof and on the side panels which advertised, "Matchbox on the Move in 1984".

SIGNBOARD ON WHEELS

The marketing efforts have been so successful that the old-time truck has been made in hundreds of different versions, with dozens of advertising or special occasion messages and a rainbow of colour combinations for its base, body and roof. In other words, Matchbox has marketed it as a little "signboard on wheels".

Matchbox itself has used the vehicle for sales and advertising messages like the time a special run of vehicles was produced as give-aways for corporate toy buyers attending the 1984 New York Toy Fair. This model, in navy, with white and yellow trim and red printing, contained the message: "Matchbox on the Move in '84". It also had a roof-top inscription, "Toy Fair '84".

The company also has made special MB38s for collectors, including the "Matchbox USA" model for Americans and the all-black 1987 model made for the second Matchbox International Collectors' Association (MICA) convention dinner. They've been produced for post offices (Isle of Man and Guernsey) and for museums (The Chester Toy Museum in England and the Power House Museum in Australia – see page 102).

Companies have used them as promotional items to be given to their own customers or, in the case of the very rare Ben Franklin vans, only 1000 were produced for the company's managers.

These workhorse-vehicles also have been issued to mark special company milestones like Reckitt & Colman's 75th anniversary celebration for Silvo Silver Polish.

The first version of the MB38 to be made by Matchbox was the blue Champion Spark Plug Van on the left. On the right is a preproduction model with a bright red finish.

COLLECTING MB38s

The first regular issue MB38 rolled down a Matchbox assembly line in 1982. This vehicle, for the 1–75 line, was the Champion Spark Plugs van. It came with royal blue cab, black base, white roof and shining chrome bumpers, headlights and grille, along with the company's familiar red and black logo incorporating a sketch of a sparkplug. Ever since, these models have been collected.

Paul Carr, author of Collecting MB38 Model A Ford Vans, points to two specific models that jump-started this specialized collecting hobby. "The first model to really trigger people's interest in the MB38s was issue 2, in February 1984, when an on-pack offer was printed on boxes of Kellogg's Cornflakes produced for the United Kingdom." Consumers who took advantage of the offer simply sent in four proofs of purchase and received a free MB38 with side panels advertising the cornflakes. The promotion lasted for six months in the United Kingdom, and was repeated in France in 1986 and in Denmark in 1987. During that extended time period, some two million vans were sent to consumers.

Not surprisingly, the Kellogg's Cornflakes MB38 is the model most widely available at swap meets, toy shows and fairs. It really put the model on the map because a normal issue of a promotional model is about 20,000 vehicles.

According to Carr, the other key version in triggering interest and making collecting of MB38s a hobby was the production of issue 20 in March 1987. Only 450 of these models were made for the 2nd MICA convention dinner and their attractive appearance, along with their limited availability, made them particularly appealing.

When White Rose Collectibles of York, Pa (see page 62) produced a two-year series of MB38s containing baseball- and football-team logos as well as the names and colours of ice-hockey and college teams, the hobby of collecting these MB38s either hit a rough road or gained new enthusiasts (depending on which collector is talking).

Some feel this series inspired new collectors of the MB38. But Carr feels differently: "The average guy had been happy buying a new model a month. But when a set of 28 football vans came out, along with another set of 26 baseball vans, two years in a row, some people either slowed down or stopped collecting for a while. They were afraid they wouldn't be able to keep their collection complete and up-to-date". But now that White Rose has moved on to other vehicles for the sporting team sets, the MB38s are moving again.

▶ **RIGHT**

Before the collecting of MB38s became popular, collecting buses was keenly pursued. In the foreground is a No 74 Daimler bus promoting "Inn on the Park". On the left is a Leyland Titan MB17-G displaying the logo "Matchbox Nurnberg 1986", while the bus on the right is a 17F Londoner.

◀ **LEFT**

The issue that probably did most to promote the idea of collecting MB38s was the package offer made by Kellogg's Cornflakes. Cornflake eaters in the UK had only to send in four tokens to receive a free MB38 decorated with the Kellogg's livery. Two million vans were distributed in the UK as well as in Denmark and France where a similar offer was made.

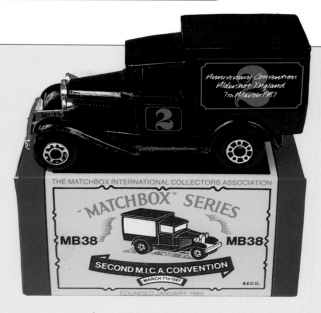

▲ **ABOVE**

This all-black van with white and blue printing is one of two versions of MB38 credited with stimulating the collecting hobby. Just 450 of these vans were made for the Matchbox International Collectors' Association. They were given away during a dinner at the second MICA convention at Aldershot, on 7 March 1987. Because this was such a limited production model, prices paid for it are always climbing.

FUTURE COLLECTORS' PRIZES

It is hard to say which models will become the most valuable, but Carr's book provides actual Matchbox production numbers for each MB38 which offer some hints. But the way in which they have been circulated is another clue. On-pack offers, according to Carr, which are quite common in the UK and very popular with overseas collectors in America and Australia, generally cost about £4. If the offer is not successful, and a company floods the market with surplus models, the value drops. At the other extreme is the limited promotion which ends with all the models gone. The value of such an issue will climb fairly quickly, both in the United Kingdom and abroad.

▲ **ABOVE**

The Ben Franklin version of the MB38, while quite valuable because so few were released (they went only to the company's management), really is quite plain. The basic white van with red roof and blue bumpers was embellished with nothing more than decals for the company which said, "Ben Franklin – Better Quality for Less".

There were two versions of the covered wagon (obviously a toy manufactured with the American market in mind). The last of the early Lesney toys, the wagons came with or without red barrels fastened to the side. The model was 5 in (12.5 cm) long, from the tip of the lead horse's muzzle to the back of the wagon. The driver even sported a bright red bandana around his neck.

▲ ABOVE
Small coronation coaches that were produced in 1953 came in silver or two shades of gold.

◄ LEFT
The miniature version of the Massey Harris Tractor, No 4, was ready for action. It had an ivory-coloured driver who was forever in his seat.

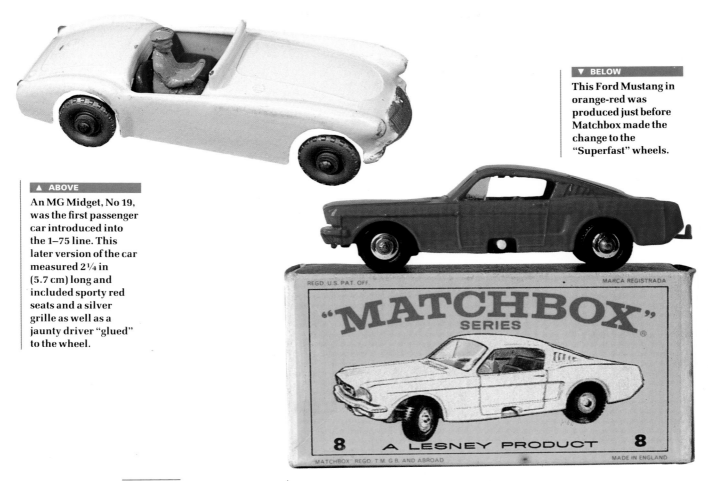

An MG Midget, No 19, was the first passenger car introduced into the 1–75 line. This later version of the car measured 2¼ in (5.7 cm) long and included sporty red seats and a silver grille as well as a jaunty driver "glued" to the wheel.

This Ford Mustang in orange-red was produced just before Matchbox made the change to the "Superfast" wheels.

THE 1–75 SERIES REGULAR WHEELS (1953–69)

The 1–75 series of Matchbox toys came into existence in 1953 and remains probably the most accessible to collectors on both sides of the Atlantic. The first three to roll off the production line were, No 1, the Aveling Barford Road Roller, No 2, the Muir Hill Site Dumper, and No 3, the Cement Mixer. Over the years, the make-up of the range has changed, with certain issues being discontinued when sales drop and other issues revamped with new bodywork. But, the number in the range has not exceeded 75 since 1980. The complicated system of numbering to identify these Matchbox toys is explained on pages 16–17.

Within the regular wheels series, a number of noteworthy vehicles exist. The MG Midget TD (19A) in 1956 became the first passenger car created for the series. Its warm reception assured Matchbox miniatures collectors that Lesney would keep new car issues rolling.

The first American vehicle was steered into the Lesney miniature line in 1957. The 31A (or 31–1), Ford Customline, sold very well. Not long afterwards, in 1959, an American Ford Thunderbird (75A) was the first car to have plastic windows from the start.

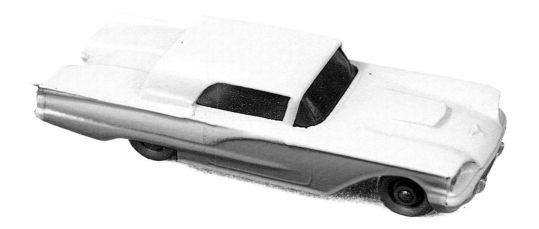

The No 75 Ford Thunderbird got off to a good start as the 1950s came to an end and the new decade was beginning. They were the first of the miniatures to have plastic windshields installed. They had varying wheel and base-plate colours but all variations were the "hot" colour combination, two-tone flesh and cream.

▶ **RIGHT**

The Atlantic tractor No 15 can be found in orange but this yellow version is much harder to locate. The yellow truck had grey wheels, a yellow trailer hitch and silver trim. Measuring 2 in (5 cm) long, it was marked "Lesney England".

◀ **LEFT**

The No 11 road tanker is hard to find in this shade of green. More common colours are red or yellow. It is 2 in (5 cm) long.

▶ **RIGHT**

The Beales Bealeson's removal van, with its tan colour, white sunburst design and white cargo door, differed greatly in appearance from the routine blue or green Pickford's vans that also were marketed as the major variations of No 46. It was also more scarce, which made it more appealing to collectors.

◀ **LEFT**

The Bedford low loader No 27, with a sky blue cab, royal blue trailer and grey wheels, is the most coveted variation of this miniature. It was marked with "British Trailer Co. Ltd." and "Made in England".

The American Ford Thunderbird was also a milestone in that the series had arrived at the number 75. Actually, there had been no firm plans to stop the series at 75, but when it arrived, the company decided to scrutinize the range to decide if any models needed replacement. At that time, it was decided that there was too heavy an emphasis on military vehicles and that there were other vehicles that were losing their appeal. Also, shop owners were beginning to get a bit nervous about the space required to display Matchbox products. Thus, Lesney began withdrawing certain models and replacing them with new ones or with new variants of existing ones.

Wheel colours and materials changed in 1958, with the switch from metal to grey and black plastic wheels. Besides giving "drivers" a better ride, the plastic variety could be made in just one step.

In 1963, the first model with opening doors, a Mercedes-Benz 220 SE coupé (53B), appeared. Next came working suspensions and "Autosteer" which allowed the car to be steered with only "simple pressure", as the pocket catalogue boasted. In 1969, an Iron Fairy Crane (42C), became the last new model to be made with regular wheels and the old gave way to the new.

▼ **BELOW**

This Aston Martin in metallic red is far rarer than its preceding colour of metallic green. This version can also have grey wheels, an even rarer variant than the black plastic ones.

▲ **ABOVE**

The No 53 Mercedes Benz 220 SE made Matchbox history because it was the first of the passenger cars to have front doors that opened. Measuring 2¾ in (6.8 cm) long, its base said "Made in England by Lesney".

▶ **RIGHT**

The No 42 Iron Fairy crane, 3 in (7.5 cm) long and first made in 1969, was the last of the new models to be made with regular, rather than Superfast, wheels.

▲ **TOP**

The hard-to-find red Ferrari Berlinetta No 75 with a white hitch came out first in a regular version (right) as well as in a Superfast wheel version (left).

▲ **ABOVE**

The underside of the Ferrari Berlinetta No 75, showing the Superfast base on the left and the regular-wheel base on the right.

A word of caution: during Lesney's heyday years, production topped about 5.5 million models per week with over 75 per cent going for export and 60 per cent of that destined for the United States. These statistics mean that when naming the rare models, what is true for one part of the world might not be true for another. Also, what the collectors of one country prize might provoke nothing more than a yawn from those of another. It is important that the novice collector finds reliable information that pertains specifically to his or her own country before setting off on the hunt.

In 1969 crisis hit Lesney. With the introduction of Mattel's Hot Wheels, Lesney was plunged into a race for survival and so developed the design for their competing Superfast wheels. As soon as possible, they began changing production from the regular wheels to the Superfast variety. Ultimately, all miniature production would be of the new type. That changeover seriously altered collecting on both sides of the Atlantic.

The differences between the two types of wheel were noticeable. The regular wheels rolled on heavy-duty 1.6 mm axles which were lodged in holes in underside projections and then "mushroomed" over in order to hold the wheels securely to the axles. The new Superfast design relied on much thinner axles that were only 0.6 mm. They had special inserts that were tailor-made to fit the bases of each different model and the wheels were formed from a special plastic that reduced the friction between the axle and the wheels and left old models standing. Not all the old models, however, could be changed over. These were either dropped or continued as they were, even after the major changeover in 1970.

In the UK, collectors essentially took the changeover to indicate that the models were indeed now toys and not for serious collecting. On the other side of the Atlantic, however, Americans greeted Superfast wheels warmly, and the collecting of the miniatures possibly even increased. Therefore, in the UK, a serious collector of miniatures almost certainly will specialize in the pre-Superfast versions, while in the USA, it will more than likely mean that both are collected.

SUPERFAST 1–75 SERIES (1969–92)

It is safe to say that the introduction of Hot Wheels by Mattel in 1969 caused Lesney to take increased notice of its American market. Sales of Matchbox nose-dived from $28 million annually to $6 million. Because most of Lesney's production was for export, and the largest single export market was the US, Lesney had no choice but to take on the American upstart face to face.

With the creation of the Superfast series, the focus of the line-up shifted. Models would change drastically. Some vehicles that were known only in the UK would be dropped in favour of models with names such as the Baja Buggy (13E), the Wildcat Dragster (8F) and the Dodge Charger (52C). Scorpions, introduced in 1971, were electrically-driven cars with rechargeable batteries.

Rola-matics were introduced in 1973. These were models that had altered Superfast wheels that turned gears which in turn operated various moving parts, such as turrets, fans, and radar antennae. Choppers motorcycles were another innovation for that year.

With the severe economic turmoil Britain experienced during 1973 and 1974, Lesney was forced to take measures that would result in some unusual issues. The coal miners' strike led to the curtailing of electricity, a three-day working week, and shortages of many industrial supplies. Lesney then decided to give some of its old paints a stir – colours that had been unpopular in the past. They also dredged up decals that had languished for years. Six Superfast models were marked with Scorpion labels (a red scorpion resting on a white circle, surrounded by a black border), even though they were not electrically powered. These models have become rare.

Hot Rods were burning out by 1975 and so were the Rola-matics. The excitement that year was for the first tampo printing appearing on a line of miniatures called "The Streakers". Tampo is the process of using a rubber pad coated with ink to print directly on the model.

Lesney began branching out in the world by producing parts to be assembled into models in Brazil in 1977, because Brazilian law made the importation of completed Lesney products very difficult. Although the venture made very little money for Lesney, the models created (often in unique colour schemes) are coveted by collectors.

They also issued special models for Germany and Japan, often using new colours on old vehicles. The earliest Japanese ones, J1 through J9, were dressed up with attractive new boxes, too.

The new decade brought more changes. New models no longer would have "Superfast" printed on their base plates. More military models were discontinued and toy safety laws were becoming more stringent. A new design for opening doors was created, one that withstood more maltreatment. Hot news, too, was the "Code Red" series of eight models for the US market that was watching the new American television programme of the same name.

With the bankruptcy of Lesney and the takeover by Universal, production was shifted to Macau and the line was split into three parts – one for the USA, one for the remainder of the world (ROW) and a CORE line of models used in both groups.

Because of the numbering changes of the models for various parts of the world, the system was becoming unworkable. A simple solution emerged to stop putting model numbers onto the bases of the 1–75 series. Boxes in which the vehicles were packed were changed, too, to include a small window. It was a distressing change for collectors because it halted the tradition of the picture box. Dealers liked the idea, however, because it meant being able to do away with the cumbersome display shelves that had showcased the models.

The year 1984 saw much activity in the models for Australia and Japan. Some recoloured models were issued for the Australian collectors' market and sold as special or limited edition models. Since then, many more such models have been produced. The Japanese line-up of vehicles would climb to 100 models by drawing on issues from other lines and ones painted just for the Japanese market.

In the UK and France, buyers were to be tempted by some hot-rod-type American models in boxes festooned with stars and stripes. As time went on, Matchbox would make many special models for everything from the James Bond movie *A View To A Kill* to Chef Boy-ar-dee canned pasta, all to sell more cars.

◄ LEFT
First produced in 1977, and measuring 4 in (10.2 cm) long, the Y-1 1936 SS 100 Jaguar offered the following baseplate information: "Lesney Products & Co. Ltd, 1977, Made in England".

▶ RIGHT

Only a handful of these AEC lorries have been found in this blue colour. The standard version was originally painted in light grey, and then later in dark grey.

▼ BELOW

This Gift Set was produced for the Australian collectors' market in the early 1980s. It was limited to a run of 5,000 pieces.

MATCHBOX CLASSIC SPORTSCARS OF THE THIRTIES MODELS of YESTERYEAR

1936 AUBURN SPEEDSTER
LIMITED EDITION No F 4884
1931 STUTZ BEARCAT

1938 MERCEDES 540K
1928 MERCEDES SS

BOOKLET CONTAINING THE COMPLETE HISTORY OF EACH CAR INSIDE.

1982 Limited Edition Pack of 5 Models

£14=78

CHIVERS & SONS LTD

Jams, Jellies, & Marmalades
THE ORCHARD FACTORY
HISTON
CAMBRIDGE

MATCHBOX

models of yesteryear

BIRD'S CUSTARD POWDER

EVANS BROS. COAL & COKE

8+YEARS. CONTAINS FIVE MODELS. 8+ANS. CONTIENT CINQ MODELES. 8+JAHRE. INHALT FÜNF MODELL.

MODELS OF YESTERYEAR

The official, and most extensive, Matchbox history refers to the Yesteryear models as Matchbox's "flagship" range. It certainly is, as far as the UK and Australia are concerned. Originally, collectors in the UK, France, Germany, and Japan were large buyers of this line, but now Australians are prepared to put down more cash to buy Models of Yesteryear than the UK and Germany combined.

Ray Bush, regarded as a world-wide authority on Matchbox because of his knowledge of the Matchbox line and his friendships with founders Leslie Smith and Jack Odell, states that in Europe, over three-quarters of collectors focus upon the Yesteryear models. US collectors, of whom three-quarters

collect the miniature 1–75 series, were probably more influenced by the fact that Fred Bronner, the man responsible for making Matchbox a household name in the USA, did very little to promote the Lesney's "flagship" line.

Collecting Models of Yesteryear has a limited following in the United States particularly as a result of recent marketing experiments and substantial price increases that have more than doubled the cost of a model. In a bid to make the model line more popular, Matchbox tried a marketing ploy that has worked well in Australia – direct marketing. The attempt failed, and the distribution of the models became even more patchy than before, though with a bit of intrepid searching the would-be collector should be able to find a supplier who can obtain virtually any current or new model.

▲ ABOVE

This 1982 limited edition pack of five Models of Yesteryear included a Y3 1912 Model T Ford Tanker marked for British Petroleum; a Y5 1927 Talbot Van in the Chivers & Sons Ltd livery; a Y-10 1906 Rolls-Royce Silver Ghost; a Birds Custard Powder Y-12 1912 Ford Model T and a Y-13 1918 Crossley truck bearing the logo of Evans Bros Coal & Coke.

SPECIFIC MODEL
ISSUE POLICY

Beginning in 1991 and announced in the pocket catalogue issued for that year, the Yesteryears and the Dinky lines became covered by Matchbox's "Specific Model Issue Policy". This policy provides that starting in 1990, each model will be recoloured only twice during its life, that any new model created from an existing one will be recoloured only once, and the most significant provision, world-wide production, will be limited.

Matchbox claims that this policy will ensure that the Yesteryears and Dinky ranges will be more collectible, the value of models will increase more rapidly, and the range will not become flooded with so many models that the collector would need to spend a fortune to collect them all. Unfortunately, this reduced volume has indeed resulted in the steep price escalation which brings problems for the buyer.

COLLECTING MODELS
OF YESTERYEAR

The line was, from its very inception, supposed to be one that appealed to adults – and especially adult collectors. It was never intended that the series should use a standard scale. Models were made to present a pleasing proportion to the eye. If that meant that a normally small road car wound up larger than an 8-ton truck, so be it. Eventually, there would be an attempt to create some uniformity within the range and detailing would be increased to distance the range from the other Matchbox lines.

Yesteryears had virtually the market to itself. Dinky and Corgi produced nothing like them. Only once was the line threatened, and that was at the inception of the Superfast programme in 1970. Several times in the line's history, collectors have created a storm of protest. The first was when Lesney began using metallic paints (as they were

▲ **ABOVE**
**The front roller of the
Aveling & Porter
Roadroller Y-11
pivots. The model is
3 in (7.5 cm) long.**

◄ LEFT

With the Goblin Electric Cleaner's logo on its panels, the Y-12 1937 GMC van was produced in 1988.

► RIGHT

This early double-decker horse-drawn bus (Y-12), marketed in 1959, offered seats out in the open as well as others under cover. The model features advertisements for Lipton's Tea as well as Hudson's Soaps and carried the bus company name: London General Omnibus Co Ltd, Victoria & King's Cross.

◄ LEFT

A welcome sight in market towns, the Guinness Y-27 Foden C-Type Steam Wagon kept pubs well-stocked with brew. But it is also a welcome addition to any collection, thanks to its attractive navy blue and gold livery with red-spoked wheels. It carries 5 barrels of beer and its base is marked "Made in Macau, Matchbox Int. Ltd". It measures 4¼ in (10.5 cm) from front to back.

► RIGHT

The Y-11 Bugatti was featured as a new car in the 1986 pocket catalogue, in the same colours as those shown here. The vehicle, 4¼ in (10.5 cm) long, was produced by Matchbox International Ltd.

◄ LEFT

The Y-5 Bentley roadster, in British racing green, sported the Union Jack on both doors. Its base inscription notes that it is a 1929 4½ litre Bentley that was made in England by Lesney.

► RIGHT

The detailing of the wood panelling on this Y-21 Ford Model A Woody Wagon of 1929 conjures up memories of country outings, one of the reasons, perhaps, why the old-fashioned station wagons are a popular collecting category in the Models of Yesteryear line. This one, in yellow and black with a red interior, carries "Made in England" and "Lesney Prod. & Co Ltd" on its base. It measures 4 in (10 cm) long and you can even read its licence plate.

doing in other lines because they had also become popular in the real car market) and when they instituted the standard use of whitewall tyres, another carryover from the other lines. Yesteryear models, shimmering in unrealistic metallic paints and with faddish whitewalls, were simply more than some serious Yesteryears collectors could stand.

Fortunately, these minor skirmishes in the history of the Models of Yesteryear have been overcome. The line has been revamped and far more attention paid to authenticity and collectability. In fact, some of those awkward, misguided touches of years ago, along with the many models that were the epitome of grace and beauty, are the very things that make the line so endearing to so many collectors.

The Yesteryears line consists of passenger cars and lorries as well as sports and racing cars, steam driven vehicles and buses and trams. The first model was an NHP Allchin Traction Engine (Y1-1), trimmed in flashy gold and copper, and with a basic livery of green with red wheels. As the years progressed, the amount of trim diminished.

The Y9-1 Fowler "Big Lion" Showman's Engine, is considered a high point in diecasting and in the Yesteryears line-up. Sold for a decade, its colour mutated from dark maroon to crimson in its final days.

Another Showman's Engine, the Y19-2 Fowler B6 that was similar in appearance, made Matchbox history because of its £18 price tag that distinguished it as the most costly Yesteryears model ever made. As somewhat of a consolation to buyers, it was sold with a card guaranteeing that the model would never again be produced.

There have been three steam locomotives in the Yesteryear range but their very small scale and lack of tenders limited their appeal. The Y13-1 Santa Fé locomotive, in light green, is coveted, however.

The Y23-1 1922 AEC Omnibus issued in 1983, encountered problems with the advertising it carried. Issued with Schweppes signage, the first red labels were unsatisfactory and new ones were ordered in black. Then Schweppes protested that there was no trademark identification and the printing was not in the company's style. A totally new design, in yellow and black, finally got the go-ahead from Schweppes. In the meantime, the few red label models that had been sold were climbing in value and some fakes appeared.

The Y16-4 1923 Scania Vabis Post Bus, issued in late 1988 to early 1989, is a curious looking contraption, with skis mounted under its front wheels and a special device enveloping the rear wheels so that the bus was driven by a continuous-loop rubber

TALBOT VAN

With the issue of the Y5-4 1927 Talbot Van, the Yesteryear line would be forever changed for it led it into the world of the promotional vehicle resulting in profits for the company and fun for the collector.

When the vehicle was first produced, it featured a Lipton's Tea logo and the Royal Crest on its side panels. The company had written to the Lord Chamberlain's office, asking to use the crest but, when no reply came by production time, they went ahead with their schedule and 100,000 had been shipped by the time official word came that permission had been denied. Lesney set about deciding what to do with the offending models while waiting to hear more from the Lord Chamberlain's office. They might have saved themselves the trouble, for news of the flap had spread and collectors scrambled to buy them up. They literally disappeared overnight. The Lord Chamberlain's office didn't require a recall, but the crest did have to be deleted from future production.

From this point on, various types of vans from Ford, Crossley, General Motors, Renault, Mack, Walker, and Morris were plastered with just about every and any conceivable logo.

Probably the most coveted Yesteryears model is the very early production of the Y4-4, a 1930 Duesenberg Model J Town Car, made in 1976. Early versions were never produced in any appreciable quantity because of problems with its looks and the casting quality.

This beautiful little Y4 Fire Engine is one of the most sought-after models of Yesteryear. It is a fragile casting and the plastic firemen are easily lost.

treadband – a system ideally suited to Sweden's snow-covered winter roads. Production of this unusual vehicle was limited to 60,000.

Through the years, various models have been added to give the line world-wide appeal. The Y10-2 1928 Mercedez-Benz 36-220, added to the range in 1963, gave new life to the company's German market, and it performed as hoped. Georges Bieber, Lesney's French importer, begged for a French car in the line and got the Y2-2 1911 Renault two-seater passenger car. America was represented by the Y7-2 Mercer Raceabout Sports Car. Racing cars by Bugatti, Ferrari, and Maserati brought Italy into the Yesteryear family.

Two models that also are favourites with collectors are the Y13-3 Ford Model T Van, produced in 1981 to celebrate the establishment of the Bang & Olufsen electronics firm, and the Y12 for the Hoover Company, in 1983. The Bang & Olufsen truck was stripped and painted white and red, with the company logo in red and the firm's name in black letters. Each one of the 750 produced, had an engraved base plate with a number corresponding to a certificate of authenticity.

The Y12s for Hoover were produced inside a special steel cage within the factory to prevent losses due to pilferage. Painted in blue with gold lettering, and printed with the Hoover motto as well as a picture of a housewife using her cleaner, the production figure for official models was 540 and an additional 20 were given to members of Lesney management. Hoover gave one to Her Majesty the Queen. The box and certificate increase the model's value greatly.

OVER 500 INTERLOCKING PIECES 16" x 20" ASSEMBLED SIZE

▼ **BELOW**
The Y-34 1933 Cadillac 452, still in its box, was among the releases for 1992, the last year the company was owned by Universal.

▲ **ABOVE**
Models of Yesteryear enthusiasts who didn't want to spend all their time buying vehicles might be tempted by this jigsaw puzzle. It contained more than 500 interlocking pieces and measured 16 by 20 in (40 by 50 cm) when completed. This collectible puzzle No 8210 was manufactured by Nordevco Inc of Plainfield, NJ.

► RIGHT

This 1912 Y-3 Model T Ford Tanker was listed as a new design in the 1989 pocket catalogue. Made by Matchbox International Ltd, it is 4 in (10 cm) long and is one of only a limited number of tankers in the range.

▼ BELOW

The Models of Yesteryear were the ornamentation for a line of giftware sold in 1960s and the early 1970s. Lesney Veteran Car Gifts, including this wooden box topped by a London Transport bus, were sold in tobacco shops, gift shops and some department stores. The only identification on the bus was an advertisement "Ah! Bisto for all meat dishes". Inside the box was the simple marking "Model by Lesney, England".

This Rolls Royce is an early example of Lesney's giftware series, still with its original box and artwork. As is often the case with collecting, the packaging can be rarer than the actual item.

Matchbox produced this specially labelled model of their Commer Van for the British Motorfair in October 1991. Only 2,500 were available, at this show or from the Matchbox International Collectors' Association.

This ashtray with a Daimler was produced in celebration of the Queen's Award to Industry, which Lesney were first awarded in 1966 and then again in 1968. It was only produced for employees of the company and was not intended for retail sale.

The very last production run of these Y7–1 Leyland lorries were fitted with black plastic wheels; all the rest had grey metal wheels.

► **RIGHT**

This Dodge Viper was to have been released in this form until a dispute arose with the cars' manufacturers. Matchbox then altered the mould completely and the car was eventually released as an entirely different vehicle known as a "Sunburner".

▼ **BELOW**

This remote-controlled Porsche was to have been a new venture for Matchbox but technical problems led to the project being abandoned at the last minute. Very few of these models have survived.

SENTRON-9 ™

PORSCHE 928 GT

FULLY ASSEMBLED 1:20 SCALE
9 CONTROL FUNCTION
STOP START
2 SPEEDS
FORWARD · REVERSE
STEERS LEFT AND RIGHT

MICRO-ELECTRONIC REMOTE CONTROL

The front cover of the 1992 pocket catalogue for collectors – the last to be produced while Matchbox was under the ownership of Universal International of Hong Kong.

DINKY

In April 1987, Universal Matchbox bought the Dinky trademark, a very well-known name in the toy business. Shortly thereafter, some Matchbox 1–75 series cars were packed and sold under the Dinky name, simply to protect the name Universal had purchased.

Because Dinky production had virtually ceased during the years before Matchbox became involved, there was no established line to keep going. Matchbox determined that the line should be similar to that of the Models of Yesteryear but with a more modern accent with cars of the 1950s and 1960s, plus an occasional one from the 1970s.

The American models in the Dinky range are the best-selling ones, except for the DY-11 and DY-11B Tucker Torpedo. Some past and present models include the DY-9B, 1949 Land Rover; the DY-21, 1964 Mini Cooper "S"; the DY-26, Studebaker Golden Hawk; the DY-25, 1958 Porsche 356A coupé; and the DY-27, 1957 Chevrolet Bel Air.

This line is intended to represent the "cars that Dad drove when I was young", and for that reason, it has been selling reasonably well. In addition to the uncertain distribution of the line, the high cost of the models helps reduce the demand for this quality line of diecast toys. For example, the size of Dinky models makes them attractive to train enthusiasts, but the high cost forces these potential customers to buy cheaper alternatives.

Collectors are individual in their collecting. There are, quite literally, dozens of other Matchbox offerings to tempt the new collector or to entice veteran collectors into branching out to new or different lines. From the King Size and SuperKings lines and the Skybusters line (a series of diecast military and commercial aircraft models) to the Gift Packs, Convoys, and the Action Sets, Matchbox has created a wonderland that appeals to the kid in everyone.

► **RIGHT**

This DY-1, 1967 Series 1½ E-Type Jaguar in racing green, was among the first cars released in 1988, after Matchbox acquired Dinky in 1987. Its front and rear licence plates were J916 and the model is 4 in (10 cm) long.

◄ **LEFT**

Matchbox decided to get some extra mileage out of vehicles in the Dinky line. In a move reminiscent of the giftware days of the 1960s and 1970s, they cast a pewter version of the 1967 Series 1½ E-Type Jaguar and mounted it on a solid wood base. Surprisingly, its wheels rotate.

► **RIGHT**

This version of DY-27 1957 Chevrolet Belair Sport Coupé is more valuable than some others because of its seat colouring.

◄ **LEFT**

A Dinky Toy Corvette was experimentally produced in pewter as a sister model to the Jaguar, but no further progress was made.

Turning on the Ignition

Getting Started in Collecting

An old saying goes that the only difference between the man and the boy is the price of the toy. When it comes to collecting Matchbox, however, one of the great things is that if you stick with new issues, the cost is the same for the man and the boy. Prices of the miniatures, for example, have not escalated as high as many other things when the increase from the early 1950s up to the present day is considered.

Recent miniatures can be purchased almost universally for well under $2 ($1.25). Even with older Matchbox pieces, prices are still in the manageable range. Very few pieces would be valued at more than $100 ($62.50); even fewer command more than $1000 ($625). In other words, while the collector is generally not going to get fantastically rich collecting Matchbox toys, neither is he going to become broke buying his collection. Perhaps this fact accounts for the great number of Matchbox collectors. More people collect diecast toys, and Matchbox in particular, than any other type of toy.

It is perhaps fortunate that not all collectors in a particular country collect the same things. For example, the two sides of the Atlantic view things quite differently. In the United States, there are many collectors who specialize in the entire 1–75 series from early Lesney days through the Superfast changeover and on to the Universal years. However, in the UK and most of Europe, the 1–75 series, especially post-Superfast models, are viewed almost exclusively as toys, and those who do collect the 1–75 series collect the older, regular-wheeled versions. For collecting, the most popular series in the UK and Europe is the Models of Yesteryear range.

Harry Rinker, a notable American antiques and collectibles expert, in his book *Collector's Guide to Toys, Games & Puzzles* propounds what he calls the "thirty year rule". This rule states that for the initial 30 years in the existence of any object, its value is purely speculative. For the object to appreciate requires three prerequisites which take thirty years to come into being. First, people must have time to throw things away, thereby reducing the number of copies of the item. Second, an item must be sold and resold, to establish its value. Finally, there must be time for people to become sentimental about objects from their childhood and to long for the lost days of youth. In addition, with advancing age comes the prosperity necessary to indulge their desires. It is not difficult to see why collecting Matchbox is increasing in popularity.

▲ ABOVE
Evidence of Matchbox efforts to sell the MB38s is clear on this model. The side panel promised "This van delivers". Judging from the number of varieties of MB38 Model A Ford vans produced (in the hundreds), no one could ever dispute the slogan. As the box stated, it was "the ideal premium".

▶ **RIGHT**
This MB38 Model A Ford Van preproduction model (with "Conventions 1982–1991" in red lettering) and the actual model (with black lettering and in the box) were produced for the Matchbox USA club. This issue, with the club's logo on the front door, was produced for the 10th annual convention held in Iselin, NJ on 8 and 9 June 1991.

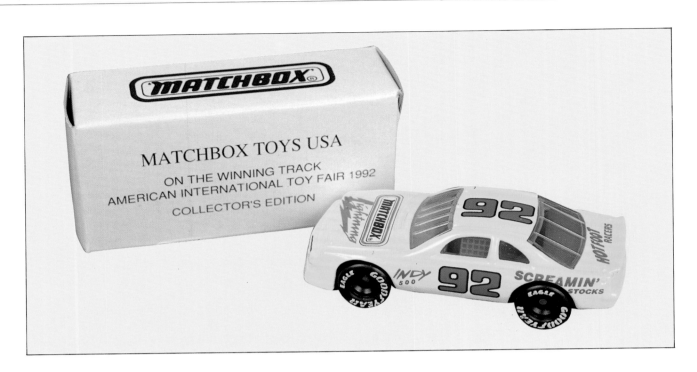

▲ TOP

Matchbox produced this Ford Thunderbird Lightning Racer as a collectors' edition for the 1992 American International Toy Fair. The base inscription said: "Ford Thunderbird. Matchbox International Limited, 1991. 1:66. Made in China".

▲ ABOVE

This Lesney Products G-8 Gift Set of vehicles from the King Size line included the K-15 Merryweather Fire Engine marked for the Kent Fire Brigade; the K-12 Foden Breakdown Tractor; the K-11 Fordson tractor and trailer and the K-1 Foden Tipper (with Hoveringham logo).

WHAT TO COLLECT

There are a number of things that any novice Matchbox collector should bear in mind when starting up. First, a neophyte collector must decide what line he or she is going to collect – the 1–75 line, Models of Yesteryear or even catalogues. Of course, in the end *anything* is collectible. Some day, people will be amazed to find that even McDonald's disposable containers might command substantial sums of money. So, don't reject a Matchbox offering because it lacks sophistication.

Remember that those items that are played with as toys, such as the 1–75 range, are most likely to disappear or become very worn, leaving the col-

lector with a rare, mint-condition collectible. On the other hand, models where almost all production immediately found its way onto collectors' display shelves which applies more to Models of Yesteryear – are all likely to survive, thereby slowing their appreciation.

Try to choose, and stick to, one particular line.

CHOOSING A LINE

The "one-of-this and one-of-that" collection mentality, especially when dealing with lines as vast as Matchbox can quickly sap the resources and enthusiasm of almost any would-be collector. A plan for collecting is essential.

▲ **ABOVE LEFT**
This King Size model Racing Porsche K101 was pictured in this tan colour in the collectors' catalogue, but apparently, few were actually marketed in this colour. They are more often found in either white or red.

▲ **ABOVE RIGHT**
The Mercury Cougar K-21 was the first of "the new fabulous King Size cars". It also had opening doors and "True Guide" steering plus an independent suspension. The off-white interior in this version is harder to find than the ones that were issued with red interiors.

▲ **ABOVE**
The K-16 articulated tanker with Quaker State livery and the slogan "Peace of Mind by the Quart", is much harder to find than some of the other versions of this truck in such liveries as Texaco, Shell or Aral.

White Rose Collectibles

If ever there were solid proof that Americans will buy diecast models specifically made for the American market, it rests in the success story of White Rose Collectibles of York, Pa (Pennsylvania). Founded in 1989, the company's growing line of products which are made by Matchbox, accounted for fully one-third of Matchbox sales in the United States by 1992.

SETTING UP WHITE ROSE

Ron Slyder, a Matchbox collector for many years, founded White Rose along with partner Chris Huber after having an inspiration while driving along a motorway. As he was driving, Slyder was passed by a NASCAR Transporter which he described as "a speeding hulk of a tractor trailer that looked like a giant box of film". Although the fast-moving vehicle quickly vanished, Slyder's mind began racing. As a Matchbox collector for nearly 20 years and proprietor of a shop that specialized in old and new Matchbox Toys, he had a good picture of what sold and what didn't sell in the diecast vehicle market. He could see their cross-market appeal to Matchbox collectors, racing fans and racing collectors.

Slyder discussed his plan with a longtime friend, Chris Huber, and the pair took action. They named their fledgling company "White Rose", taken from the nickname of the Pennsylvanian city in which they were establishing their company. Their appeal would be to collectors, rather than to toy buyers, which is why they added "Collectibles" to the company name.

Their first step was to determine whether Matchbox would make the models for them. They got an affirmative nod from the company but realized they would need to work out licensing agreements with the NASCAR teams. On the road with their sales pitch, their first stop was the Hardee's Racing Shop where they met with Cale Yarbrough and his team manager, Bob Tomlinson. Then they went onto Sports Image and Hendrick's Motorsports before they made a final stop to meet Richard Petty. Yarborough showed them how a NASCAR team runs and the White Rose founders got his permission to do a Hardee's transporter and Petty, a Matchbox collector himself, gave the go-ahead to include the racing team in their plans.

That first year, they managed to produce four Superstar Transporters: the Dale Earnhardt Goodwrench Racing Team Transporter; the Richard Petty STP Racing Transporter; Cale Yarborough's Hardee's Racing Transporter and the Neil Bonnett Citgo Racing Transporter.

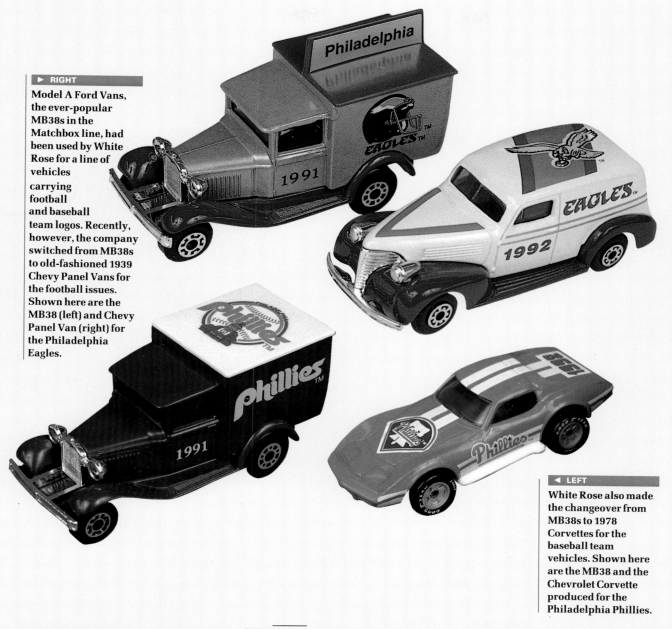

▶ RIGHT
Model A Ford Vans, the ever-popular MB38s in the Matchbox line, had been used by White Rose for a line of vehicles carrying football and baseball team logos. Recently, however, the company switched from MB38s to old-fashioned 1939 Chevy Panel Vans for the football issues. Shown here are the MB38 (left) and Chevy Panel Van (right) for the Philadelphia Eagles.

◀ LEFT
White Rose also made the changeover from MB38s to 1978 Corvettes for the baseball team vehicles. Shown here are the MB38 and the Chevrolet Corvette produced for the Philadelphia Phillies.

◀ LEFT
The White Rose line of NASCAR vehicles including superstar transporters, three-piece team convoys and racing cars have cross-market appeal to both racing as well as Matchbox enthusiasts. The York, Pennsylvania, company focused on the Dale Earnhardt Goodwrench Racing Team for a number of its earliest Code 1 vehicles (made by Matchbox, for White Rose).

OTHER WHITE ROSE LINES

The NASCAR vehicles are White Rose's best-known products but among other products in its line have been two years' of Matchbox MB38 Model A Ford vans bearing baseball and football team logos. Now, however, Slyder and Huber have switched from the MB38 to a 1939 Chevy panel truck (MB245) for their most recent line of football team vehicles and Corvettes for the baseball team vehicles. Nevertheless, the original Superstar Transporter Series remains the company's most popular, and most collected, line.

White Rose sales really got under way in 1990. As collectors clamoured

for the newest transporters, two additional series were launched, the company's first three-piece Convoy and the first single Lumina car, both carrying the Goodwrench racing team logos.

White Rose's strategy of producing top-quality, limited-production models has been seen to work. The transporters and the rest of the NASCAR line are sold primarily through racing outlets and Matchbox speciality shops, and sometimes are sold out.

White Rose models are recognized for their top-quality designs and the fine tampo printing. It takes a fine degree of skill to print four colours in the correct space so that each colour is right and there is no overprinting.

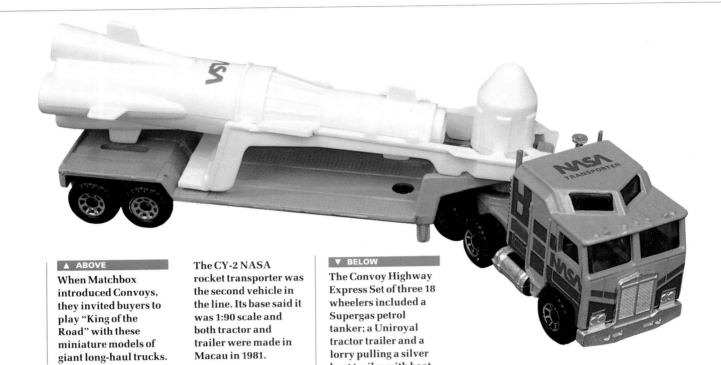

▲ ABOVE
When Matchbox introduced Convoys, they invited buyers to play "King of the Road" with these miniature models of giant long-haul trucks.

The CY-2 NASA rocket transporter was the second vehicle in the line. Its base said it was 1:90 scale and both tractor and trailer were made in Macau in 1981.

▼ BELOW
The Convoy Highway Express Set of three 18 wheelers included a Supergas petrol tanker; a Uniroyal tractor trailer and a lorry pulling a silver boat trailer with boat.

START WITH WHAT IS CURRENT

Most established collectors agree that a good place to start is with what is current in your chosen line and then keep up with new issues as they are made available. Then, with your collection under way, you might want to start looking at, and for, previous models in your chosen line, buying when a desired model is found at a good price. However, do bear in mind that increasing age and scarcity breed price increases, so start filling in the gaps in your line from previous models as soon as possible and so help keep down the cost of your collection.

Society in general has become more "collectible conscious" in the past several years. A local auctioneer was recently bemoaning the fact that "everyone's an expert. People know the value of things in general so there are many fewer incredible bargains any more." Media hype concerning collectibles has convinced some people to become speculators in the collectibles market. But these people are out to make quick money in the shortest possible time, generally about five to ten years. Their plans might work if the number of speculators in a certain type of collectible is small. But if there are many people collecting, the release onto the market of those items will cause the values to drop precipitously.

Essentially what all of this means is that the market for any collectible is controlled by the answer to one question: How many of the item were made? While it might seem to be an easily answered question, it isn't. Matchbox and Lledo, like most companies, guard their production figures with all the ironclad security of Pentagon secrets. There-

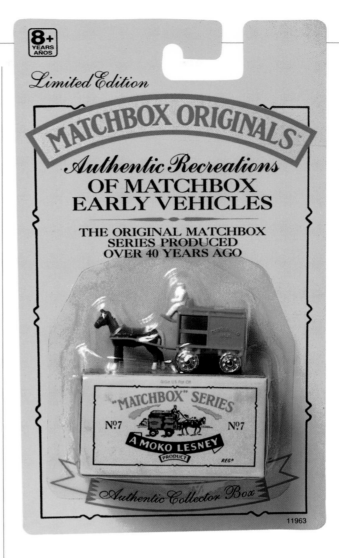

▲ ABOVE
Matchbox acknowledged the importance of the collectors' market in 1992 by re-issuing these early models. The castings are, however, new and should not be confused with the 1950s issues.

fore, the collector is at a disadvantage. There can be speculation, and an occasional insider who might leak information, but the vast majority of these statistics are never revealed.

Be wary of production figures and proclamations of "limited editions". First of all, if a model is especially popular, the temptation is there on the part of the company for another release. While a catalogue or publication might list a number produced, that number could be wrong even before the number is published. At one point, a book quoted a figure of 5000 for a specific Lledo model. Jack Odell, the Chairman, just to check the figure, sat down at his desk and computed that with re-orders, the number produced was probably closer to 25,000.

Also, in almost every area of collecting, there is usually someone sitting on a stash of items through which he hopes to control the market by careful

◄ LEFT
For motorcycle enthusiasts, Matchbox has been producing Hot Rider Tour Bikes. These Harley-Davidson motorbikes were first sold in 1992 in red and blue, with lots of silver and gold trim to glisten as they headed down the road.

▲ ABOVE

Since Skybusters were first introduced by Matchbox in 1973, there are few planes that have not been recreated as diecast miniatures. Clockwise from the left are: a British Airways Boeing 747 (SB10); an SB12 Pitts Special in blue and white with the Matchbox logo on the wings; a Hind/D Soviet heavy assault helicopter; the SB26 Cessna 210G pontoon plane like the one used by 007 James Bond in the movie "Living Daylights" and an F117A Stealth Bomber (SB36).

▼ BELOW AND
OPPOSITE BOTTOM

Sea Kings, a line of diecast ships, was conceived by Lesney Products in 1976. But they were dragging their anchors from the start. They barely left the dock, let alone got up to full speed, with collectors. The K304 Aircraft Carrier with four planes on deck; a preproduction model of a Texaco supertanker that was never launched and the K309 submarine that was made in 1978, the same year the Matchbox fleet was "mothballed".

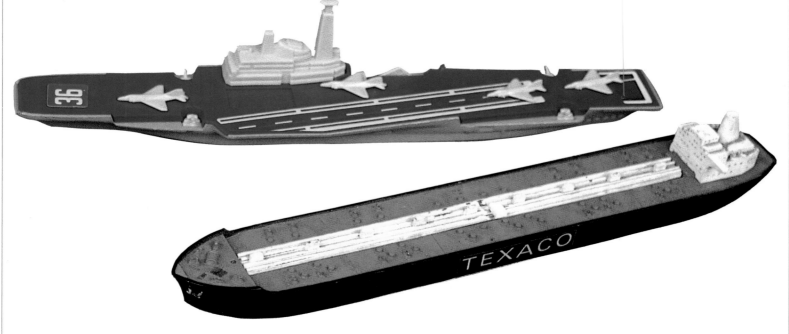

release. These "suppliers" wield fearsome power and command respect, though it is likely to be the grudging variety from other collectors. Many collectors discover, to their chagrin, that dealing with such people becomes almost a necessity because they have what no one else does. Some collectors even guard the existence of such people, almost as if letting outsiders or newcomers know would be giving away trade secrets or tempting fate.

Of course, a huge release onto the market would lower the value of everyone's collection, including the person who had released it, so it is in the best interests of the hoarders to act responsibly.

If serious collecting is the goal, especially the collecting of the older models, these "suppliers" need to be found by a bit of old-fashioned sleuthing, for it is they who will be able to supply virtually all that is necessary and sometimes at prices that are actually lower than those of other small collectors. The question that now naturally arises is, "How do I go about finding such 'suppliers'?" The answer to this question leads directly to the first rule of collecting.

▲ ABOVE

How many roads can Matchbox designers take? This limited display of the obvious variations made from one basic model gives an idea of how complex and detailed Matchbox collecting can be. The 25 variations of Mod Rod No 1, with "1971 Made in England" on the base, fills the better part of a shelf at the Matchbox Road Museum in Newfield, NJ. This picture shows a sampling of the more obvious differences – shades in a single body colour, completely different body colours (see silver model in the foreground), decaling differences and differences in wheel and engine colour. Collectors who really go in for detail sometimes will search for different axle finishes and different wheel treads and shades of difference in the plastic used for windshields.

Gift Sets

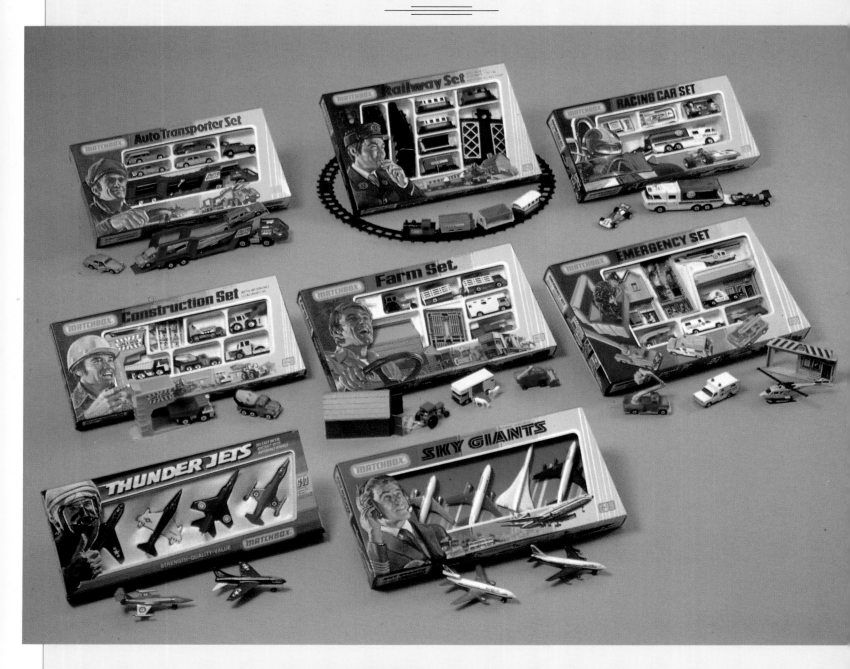

▲ ABOVE

Giftsets! Someone decided to market them in a big way in the late 1970s and early 1980s. This photograph of assortments of diecast vehicles, grouped according to a common theme, includes: a car transporter set; a railway set; a racing car set; a construction set; a farm set; an emergency set; Thunder Jets; and Sky Giants. Matchbox had come a long way from the early days when vehicles were randomly combined in gift sets that had no common thread other than their manufacture by Matchbox.

▲ **TOP**

The Construction Set G-5 in 1979 included a Load-a-Vator for loading rocks, sand and gravel; a dump truck, a cement mixer, a bulldozer, a shovel-nose tractor and a Bomag road roller.

▲ **ABOVE**

Complete with plastic-fronted accessories made to look like a hospital entrance, the front of a burning building and the front of a police station, the Emergency Set G-7 for 1979 included two types of fire engines (a snorkel fire engine No 13 and a Blaze Buster), an ambulance, a police car and a rescue helicopter and two emergency personnel.

▲ **TOP**
Farm Set G-6 included a tractor with plough, a combine harvester, a red lorry and red trailer for transporting cattle and a horsebox.

▲ **ABOVE**
The G-6 Drag Race Set was among gift sets featured in 1972. It contained six Superfast cars along with a Thunderbolt Launcher and launch extension.

▲ ABOVE

Action Pack G-5 featured five vehicles marked with the Federal Express livery. It was advertised as "new" in the 1987 Matchbox pocket catalogue.

▲ **ABOVE**

This two-storey garage was available to fleet owners in 1959. These models are actually quite hard to find today as the plastic parts were easily broken or lost. The boxes they came in are perhaps even more difficult to locate.

▲ **ABOVE**

This Car Ferry was a
novel and popular
product designed to
add more play value
to the standard range
of diecast cars. It was
available in several
colour schemes and
the choice of cars
could vary. The most
easily found set is
shown here.

▲ **ABOVE**

This car dealer's lot
dates from the early
1970s. It is important
to remember that all
the pieces should be
complete and
included when buying
an item such as this.
The model cars were
not included in the set.

▲ ABOVE
the 1969 catalogue came in two editions with only subtle differences between them. "Autosteer" was the big news that year. It was a feature that enabled the cars' front wheels to be turned right or left by applying pressure to the car. The front cover illustration must have been a little disconcerting for Americans reading the USA editorial where driving on the left isn't a way of life.

FINDING OUT ABOUT YOUR COLLECTION – BOOKS

Knowledge is your first and foremost foundation. Upon it all of your collecting activities will be built. Too little knowledge can cause the crumbling of your pastime into a collection that costs too much and is worth too little.

The first building block of your foundation is books. Many books are available on the collecting of Matchbox cars, and many more are being planned and written at this moment.

Books available are numerous and varied, and many more are being readied for the market. The major ones are described below.

A very helpful book for the beginning collector of any toy line is Harry Rinker's *Collector's Guide to Toys, Games & Puzzles* (Radnor, Pa: Wallace-Homestead Book Company, 1991). For general information, advice, warnings, and just plain common sense, this book is a veritable gold mine. Time spent digging into its pages will, in the long run, save countless hours.

Certainly the largest, most comprehensive, and most attractive book on Matchbox was issued as part of its 40th anniversary. It is titled *Collecting Matchbox Toys – The First Forty Years* by Kevin McGimpsey and Stewart Orr (Chester, England: Major Productions, 1989). The first edition was printed in May 1989 and consisted of only 7200 copies. It is available directly from Matchbox and from some dealers. A first edition copy includes a special certificate certifying it as such.

Charlie Mack, who easily qualifies as "Mr Matchbox" in the USA and also is the head of the largest US Matchbox collectors' club, has produced a number of important volumes on the various Matchbox ranges. An up-to-date look at the early

Matchbox toys is provided in *Lesney's Matchbox® Toys – Regular Wheel Years, 1947–1969* (West Chester, Pa: Schiffer Publishing, 1992). The full-colour volume does contain a price guide, which gives the values in ranges. It also points out those models that are rare and those that are not.

In addition, Mack authored *Matchbox Models of Yesteryear™* (Durham, Ct: Matchbox USA, 1989). And he is currently working on two more books. The first one will be a book covering the Superfast years (1969–82) and another will chronicle the Universal years (1982–92). Both volumes should be issued during 1993 and will be published by Schiffer Publishing of West Chester, Pennsylvania.

Dr Edward Force penned *Matchbox and Lledo Toys*, a book that is a combination of an older Matchbox-Lledo price guide and variations list. Again, mostly in full colour, it covers modern Matchbox production of the 1–75 series, Dinky, Superfast Specials, Twin Packs, Models of Yesteryear, Convoy, SuperKings and some other limited production special lines. He attempts to give both the UK and the US model numbers, but as his introduction points out, it is not a complete listing but rather a compilation of the major variations.

A detailed, complete price guide book mostly with the UK market in mind was written by Frank Thompson: *The Matchbox Toy Price Guide (3rd Edition)* (London: AC Black, 1990). This book covers the entire production of Matchbox toys, souvenir items and catalogues, from 1953 until 1990. The book is a wealth of detailed information about the various models arranged by type and number, but because there are very few pictures, and those that are used are in black and white, the book is valuable only after the owner or prospective purchaser knows the range code and model number. The guide gives prices for "mint boxed", "mint unboxed" and "good condition". Thompson's book is especially good for determining which models in the various ranges (especially the Yesteryears Code 2 models) are the rarest and most valuable. The author travels around the UK in his Atlantean Double Decker Bus Museum filled with a 30-year collection of Matchbox toys.

Paul Carr, a recently-retired employee of sixteen years of the Matchbox Research and Design Department, has produced a book entitled *Collecting MB38 Model A Ford Vans*. Copies of the book are available by writing to Carr at Unit D–10, The Seedbed Centre, Langston Road, Loughton, Essex IG10 3TQ, UK.

Philip Bowdidge has published a number of booklets about Matchbox collecting, again with mostly the UK in mind. The illustrations are in black and white, and the information they present could be helpful to the collector. His works deal mostly with the 1–75 range, the Major Packs, and the Accessory Packs. Bowdidge is one of the few sources of detailed information about Matchbox boxes in which various lines of Matchbox toys were packed. While some collectors claim to be collecting just the boxes, more likely those collectors are really serving as sources of boxes for those collectors who need the original box to complete a certain model of their collection. It is a fact that the collected models have a higher value if they are accompanied by their original boxes. According to Frank Thompson, one collector made over £6000 in years 1980–81 through the sale of empty boxes alone. In the UK, the early Lesney boxes for the 1–75 series and the boxes for the Models of Yesteryear are in the greatest demand. In addition, Bowdidge has produced a booklet on the Matchbox catalogues between 1957 and 1990. His works can be secured by writing to Mr Bowdidge at 8 Melrose Court, Ashley, New Milton, Hants, BH25 5BY, UK.

Specifically for catalogues, an American collector, Lt Col James W Smith (US Army Ret), 431 George Cross Drive, Norman, Ok 73069 USA has produced a 68-page photocopied listing showing pictures of all of the catalogues that have been issued, descriptions of their differences, and summaries of those published in languages other than English.

PRICE GUIDES

Many of these volumes contain price guides which aim to help the collector know what various models are worth. Price guides are grudgingly seen as necessities; no collector really likes them, but at one time or another, every collector – especially the novice – needs them. By the time price guides are written and printed, they are mostly out of date, generally by at least a year. The collectibles markets can be very mercurial, and the nature of book production and publishing makes for difficulties in reflecting up-to-date market realities. Also price guides sometimes try to set prices, rather than reflect them. If a price given in a guide is high, market prices can rise to meet it; and this is sometimes the goal of the collector and/or dealer who has written the guide. On the other hand, if a price in a guide is much lower than the current price on the market, it could actually drive the market price down.

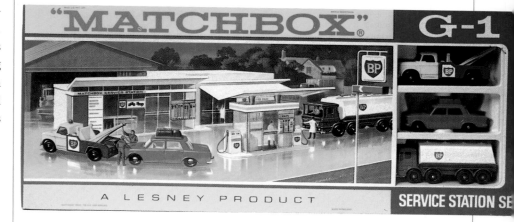

▼ **BELOW**
The Big MX range was an unsuccessful attempt by Matchbox to provide vehicles which were mechanised. The range consisted of standard models which had been converted and, incidentally, re-coloured. This Tractor Transporter had an operating winch. The tractors were painted orange instead of the usual blue.

▲ **ABOVE**
Matchbox rarely produced models in colours that were not available individually, but the Fiat 1500 illustrated here is the exception. Normally it was painted in pale green, which makes this red version very hard to find.

▲ **TOP**
At first glance, these Coca Cola delivery vans look identical, but each model sports different wheels. Examine also the crates of bottles. The first version has unevenly stacked crates but the other two do not.

FAKES

Fraudulent models can be problems for even the seasoned Matchbox collector because Matchbox production is and was so assorted that it would be very difficult for any collectors' guide to show or list all the variations produced either by Lesney or by Universal Matchbox. Even factories in Bulgaria and Hungary were churning out models that were coloured according to their markets and tastes. Models were also produced in Brazil, again according to local tastes. Obviously, with Matchbox activities in over 144 countries and actual production going on in some of those, creating any guide that would (or could!) list all of them is nearly impossible.

In one particularly notorious scam, unscrupulous dealers took Lledo's first DG-5 model, a horse-drawn fire engine and selling at the time for about £2, and filed off the Lledo name from the base and repainted it red. In London's Petticoat Lane, they hawked it as the original Lesney

Yesteryears horse-drawn fire engine which, at the time, was selling for about £175. A truly knowledgable collector would have known that the Days Gone series from Lledo is slightly smaller than the Lesney Yesteryears. Knowledge is the foundation – remember?

This unauthorised copy of Matchbox Y12–3 serves to highlight how much better the real thing is. Made in Poland in about 1984, it is made entirely of plastic.

DECORATION

Imperfections in painting and transfer work make a model unacceptable to one collector and yet more desirable to another. For example, a transfer or decal can be placed upside down on a vehicle. In fact, this occurrence was fairly common, as author-ized outworkers, sometimes non-English speaking, were hired at times to do specialized painting and transfer work. Lesney then had a difficult time making sure that all of the models were identical when issued. One Yesteryears model, the Y6-D 1920 Rolls-Royce Fire Engine, had the transfers affixed upside down on all of its very early produc-tion. The same applies to early Lledo production.

GETTING TO KNOW THE MARKET

How does a novice collector start getting to know the market? The answer is first join a few clubs and organizations and then start travelling to toy shows, swap meets, meetings of collectors' clubs, club con-ventions, Matchbox museums and toy shops.

CODE SYSTEM

In response to the problem of models being repainted and altered to look like rare ones, Ray Bush created the still-used code system for classi-fying Matchbox and Lledo models. It is a system of three categories – Codes 1, 2 and 3 – that are used to identify real and ersatz Matchbox models.

A Code 1 vehicle is one that was completely pro-duced by Lesney or its successor. That includes all decoration such as labels, decals, and tampo print-ing. Because Matchbox does all the work (making and detailing) on White Rose models, they are Code 1. Code 2 is one that was altered by a third party but with the complete written approval of the Lesney or Matchbox management. Code 3 is a nor-mal Lesney or Matchbox model that was changed in colour, design, or decoration without the knowl-edge or approval of Lesney or Matchbox. In itself, nothing is wrong with Code 3 samples provided they are clearly marked or represented as Code 3. Some collectors even specialize in collecting Code 3 models.

MICA

The Matchbox International Collectors' Association (MICA) began in January 1985, taking the place of the UK Matchbox Club which folded up in that year. It has evolved into an extremely large, well-organized operation that produces six bi-monthly magazines per year. The magazine, in full colour, frequently runs articles on Yesteryears models; early, rare regular wheel and Superfast models; articles on catalogues; readers' news and views; listings of upcoming collectors' fairs and meets; news from the Australian and USA Matchbox markets; and a classified ad section. The Association also holds annual conventions, attended by collectors from all over the world. New members are welcome. Send a stamped, addressed envelope (sae) or two International Reply Coupons (IRCs) to the local representative of the club.

USA and Canada: The Membership Secretary, MICA North America, 585 Highpoint Avenue, Waterloo, Ontario, Canada N2L 4Z3.

UK and Europe: The Membership Secretary, MICA; 13 Lower Bridge Street, Chester CH1 1RS, UK.

Australia and New Zealand: MICA Co-Ordinator; Matchbox Toys Pty Ltd, 5 Leeds Street, Rhodes, Sydney, NSW 2138, Australia.

Matchbox USA

In the USA, the Matchbox USA club offers twelve monthly magazines (with black and white photographs) which stress the miniatures and Yesteryears ranges but which also run articles on other Matchbox offerings over the years. If it has the name Matchbox on it, it could find its way into this publication. Even the new issues of the "Monster in My Pocket" are catalogued. Again, the magazine contains a classified section for swapping and selling. Charlie Mack is the head of this organization, which numbers about 1500 members worldwide, and the publisher of the club's magazine. The address of the club is Matchbox USA, Rural Route 3, Box 216, Saw Mill Road, Durham, Connecticut 06422, USA. Again, enclose an sae or two IRCs.

Mack oversees another Matchbox Collectors' Club that originally ran from 1966 to 1982 and reformed in 1989, and has a newsletter issued quarterly. Write to Charles Mack at PO Box 278, Durham, Ct 06422, USA.

One of the few surviving small clubs is the Pennsylvania "Matchbox" Collectors' Club. It holds regular meetings at various members' homes throughout the year and also actively attends shows and meets throughout the Pennsylvania-New York-Maryland areas. It publishes the *Pennsylvania Matchbox Newsletter*, which provides limited information about new releases. The club also pays some attention to the collecting of Lledo models. Membership in the club is open to all and can be obtained by writing to William J. Charles, 2015 Old Philadelphia Pike, Lancaster, Pa 17602, USA.

American International Matchbox Inc (AIM) was founded in May 1970 by Harold Colpitts of Lynn, Massachusetts. The club expanded and eventually included chapters in Massachusetts, Connecticut, and Maryland. Still in operation today, it offers yearly and half-yearly memberships. For membership details, write to American International Matchbox Inc, 532 Chestnut St, Lynn, Ma 01904, USA.

For Lledo Collectors

For Lledo collectors, there is a magazine, *Lledo Calling*, and an international Lledo club. Produced by RDP Publications, there are five newsletters a year that provide information about both Days Gone and promotional models and information concerning souvenir models. They also contain advertisements about models that are for sale. *The Days Gone Collector*, a second magazine also available from Ray Dowding, contains information about the Days Gone models. This publication is issued four times a year. For information about either or to suscribe write to the New Subscriptions Department, PO Box 1946, Halesowen, West Midlands B63 3TS, UK.

CONDITION OF YOUR MATCHBOX

The proliferation of price guides has also had another unfortunate effect on the collectibles markets. People sometimes, by seeing a price printed in a price guide, get the mistaken impression that the Matchbox toys they played with as children are somehow worth these rarefied prices. In fact such high prices are reserved for those referred to as MB, which stands not for Matchbox but for "mint boxed".

Theoretically, a mint condition toy is one that has no imperfections of any sort, but in reality, it means that the model has not been played with and has minimal evidence of scratches and fading. Because Matchbox toys were mass-produced, not all models were perfect when they left the factory and, as most of them were packed in boxes, this led to a bit of scuffing in transit, in some cases, halfway around the world.

In short, when dealing with price guides, the collector has to be sceptical and careful. Remember that the prices listed in the guide are retail, not wholesale, and if the guide is used as the basis for a sale to a dealer, the dealer will need a markup on the item in order to make it worth his while to resell it.

INVESTMENT FOR THE FUTURE – DISNEY SERIES

If you're looking to make an investment for the future, most collectors are betting that the Matchbox Disney series, produced by Universal Toys of Hong Kong (before Universal bought Matchbox), have the potential to increase significantly in value. Really directed at children, the line got its start in 1979 and came to a halt in 1980.

The sheer joy with which Matchbox announced the arrival of these characters that have always captured the imagination of children, was apparent in 1979's pocket catalogue. Across the tops of pages 36 and 37, copy writers used the word "NEW" in large letters, eight times. The line began with WD-1 (Mickey Mouse piloting a fire engine); WD-2 (Donald Duck driving a beach buggy); WD-3 (Goofy cruising in a Beetle); WD-4 (Minnie Mouse touring in a Lincoln); WD-5 (Mickey in a Jeep); WD-6 (Donald Duck driving a police Jeep). The catalogue noted that an additional three models (WD-7 (Pinocchio's Road Show); WD-8 (Jiminy Cricket's Old Timer) and WD-9 (Goofy's Racer), would be available in late 1979.

The 1980/81 catalogue, only slightly less emphatic in its sales pitch about still more "NEW!" models showed an additional three models: WD-10 (Goofy's Train); the WD-11 (Donald Duck driving an ice cream truck) and the last of the Disneys, the WD-12 (Mickey driving a Corvette).

In the 1981/82 Matchbox catalogue, the company expanded into the Popeye series (copyright King Features Syndicate, Inc). The CS-13 was Popeye's spinach truck; the CS14 Bluto's Road Roller and CS15 Olive Oyl's sports car.

Two things have made the line particularly appealing to collectors as one to buy and save. First of all, since they were sold as toys, many will have been scratched and damaged, greatly reducing the number of "mint condition" models available, and therefore, increasing the price for them. Secondly, these models appeal to both Matchbox collectors and Disney collectors. The greater the number of potential buyers, and the fewer the number of mint models available, the more this Wonderful World of Disney takes on a wonderful glow for collectors.

◄ LEFT
In 1980, Matchbox announced, "The Success Story Continues" and photographed Goofy in his train, Donald driving the ice cream truck and, the last of the line, Mickey in his sporty red Corvette.

▼ BELOW
Goofy managed to come out with three different vehicles – as many as the scene-stealing mouse. Here he is shown (left) in the earliest Goofy model, a Beetle (WD-3), in his sports car (WD-9) and, finally, in his train (WD-10).

▲ ABOVE
A closeup shows Mickey in his fire engine (WD-1); Minnie in her Lincoln (WD-4) and Donald, ready to break it up, in his white police Jeep (WD-6).

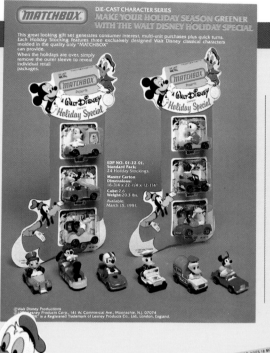

◀ LEFT
▼ BELOW

Ingenious bits of marketing were these Christmas stockings each containing three blister-packed Disney characters. If they didn't sell by the time the holidays had come and gone, all a retailer had to do was pop them out of the stocking and sell them in their still-perfect blister packs.

◀ LEFT

This advertisement shows those models released in late 1979, with a background of models already on the market. As Matchbox copywriters noted: "Our family is growing with three new characters from Walt Disney and Matchbox". They were colourfully finished and raced on Superfast wheels.

▲ TOP

This 1981 shop display unit shows the Popeye line, with Olive Oyl (left) in a white convertible, Popeye in his spinach truck and Bluto at the wheel of a road roller.

Road Maps Across Time

Matchbox Pocket Catalogues

"MATCHBOX" COLLECTOR'S CATALOGUE | 1965 International Edition

▲ **ABOVE**
The 1965 edition had a front cover appealing to racing enthusiasts.

P aging through old Matchbox catalogues is like following a road map across time. They steer readers past page after page of each era's most popular passenger vehicles, forever preserved in sketches or photographs. They provide glimpses of construction, farm and emergency vehicles that helped shape the world. As well as the past and the Models of Yesteryear, they try to depict the future (with issues like Matchbox 2000).

LEARNING TO USE POCKET CATALOGUES

Although there is a temptation to regard these catalogues as gospel, those who are familiar with the actual Matchbox products know better. Models depicted on the pages were not always what Matchbox finally produced, because catalogue copy needed to be set long before some new models were rolling along the assembly line.

Sometimes, the catalogue sketches or photographs were coloured differently than the final product. Sometimes, the vehicles and playsets the catalogues labelled as "expected by mid year" didn't make it onto the market until months later, if at all. And not everything in every catalogue was available worldwide. Nevertheless, the catalogues help tell the company's story, both through reports and photographs, as well as with subtle messages conveyed between the lines.

ENCOURAGING SALES

Over the years, obviously, these catalogues have encouraged and, at times, exhorted collectors of all

ages to buy more Matchbox toys. Early catalogues contained special blanks next to listings for, say, the 1–75 models, along with the question: "Are these models in your collection? You can tick them off as you buy." As if that wasn't enough encouragement, a few catalogues also contained a special month-by-month chart that enthusiasts could use to keep a running inventory of their collections as well as the future purchases they planned to make.

NEW MODELS AND CHANGES

Catalogues usually contained a list of new models and repaints, either before or after the listings for each major line, or indicated changes and new additions with special asterisks within the basic listings. Information on Matchbox accessories, from carrying cases and car washes to car parks and road systems, is also provided by these pocket catalogues.

Sporadically, there have been summaries of changes in 1–75 and Models of Yesteryear series for specific decades, although a better look at this comes from examining current Matchbox price guides.

MINES OF INFORMATION

But Matchbox catalogues have provided much more than the basic information a person needed to buy new vehicles. The 1968 catalogue even records how the paper was made for the catalogue. Indeed early catalogues provided interesting bits of information for enthusiasts, rewarding them with the inside scoop. With every purchase, buyers were

Announced and promoted in the 1967 catalogue was the Ford Mustang Fastback No 8, which measured 2⅞ in (7 cm). The car was the first to contain working steering that operated by pressing the bar at the base of the driver's door. In this catalogue, mention was made of how well the regular full-size Mustang by Ford was selling. But the catalogue added that this Matchbox version had surely outsold the real vehicle since more than a million models had been shipped worldwide in the few weeks following its introduction into the range.

made to feel they were taking stock in the company.

The 1966 catalogue, which detailed how Matchbox models were made, told readers that more than 3600 people played a part in a great team with the highest score in the world – over 100 million models made and sold per year.

Once there was a quiz to goad collectors, testing them on information like:

"From which country comes the full-size version of the famous Models of Yesteryear No Y16 Spyker"? (Answer: Holland.)

"Why is the prototype of the very famous Models of Yesteryear No Y15 Rolls-Royce called a 'Silver Ghost'"? (Answer: The original car was so silent and smooth in its day that the manufacturer christened it the "Ghost". The first "Ghosts" were in a beautiful polished silver finish and soon became known as "Silver Ghosts".)

And, finally, "Who is the world's greatest manufacturer of motor vehicles?"

Anyone who didn't answer "Matchbox" to that last question had a problem, particularly if the same person missed six or more questions in the whole quiz. A person who scored nearly 9 of 10 correct answers was declared a "Five-Star top-class Matchbox model expert".

READING BETWEEN THE LINES

In 1970, after being forced by Mattel's success in the US with Hot Wheels to consider seriously the company's own future, catalogue copy writers also speculated about future vehicles and the role Matchbox would play.

They wrote: "What will cars of the future be like? Obviously low, with aerodynamic styling. Plastic will be used increasingly for body shells. Motorways would have wires beneath their surfaces to instruct the car what to do. Programmed journey cassettes could be slotted into the dashboard, leaving the driver to enjoy the view. Cars could even dispense with wheels altogether and travel on a thin cushion of air, using compressed air for power. The Wankel rotary engine and gas turbine engines have been tried and proved. In the not too distant future, cars may rely on atomic energy as a course of power. Matchbox, as always, will continue to keep pace with tomorrow – today!"

Matchbox had to convey the image that it was really moving after the success of Mattel's Hot Wheels sent Matchbox designers back to the drawing board. The cover and inside pages of this catalogue were designed to impart a feeling of motion. It was brimming with accessories for the new Superfast vehicles created by Matchbox to compete with Mattel.

SF-4 DOUBLE LOOP
RACE SET
A LESNEY PRODUCT

TECHNICAL DETAILS

New design accomplishments were heralded in these catalogues, and the best example of this is the 1970 issue which carried the first notice of the Superfast models. What you see here is Matchbox's reaction to the success of Mattel's Hot Wheels in 1969.

The importance of the Superfast line to Matchbox was indicated on practically every page, including the cover which contained the word "Superfast" surprinted over a rolling wheel.

The Superfast theme was carried through the catalogue with the vehicle illustrations (sketches because many of the models were still on the drawing board) which convey a feeling of movement and speed of the new "Superfast 1–75 series" moving on the open road.

Copy for Superfast models was designed to get a speed demon's blood running. "See them roaring down the track, hanging upside down on the loop-the-loop, clinging grimly to the banked tracks at incredible speeds", and so on.

At the start of the 1–75 catalogue section, writers went even further: "Think of the fun you will have in matching a Lamborghini Miura against a bus, or a fire engine against a refuse truck. That's racing with a difference – Superfast style". It was different all right. A bus is hardly a worthy racing adversary for a Lamborghini and a refuse truck is seldom envisioned as a racing vehicle.

▲ ABOVE

The SF-4 Double Loop Race Set was one of the accessories advertised in the 1970 catalogue. According to the copy, a child could throw the starting lever and then watch two cars complete the loops and streak neck and neck towards the finishing gate.

◄ LEFT

The colourful 1967 collectors' catalogue, displaying the flags of some of the company's best customers on the front and back covers, had an international theme. It described how vehicles journeyed to get from Lesney to buyers all over the world and announced "working steering" for the first time in a Matchbox miniature. According to a diagram within the catalogue, pushing a lever by the driver's door directed the wheels.

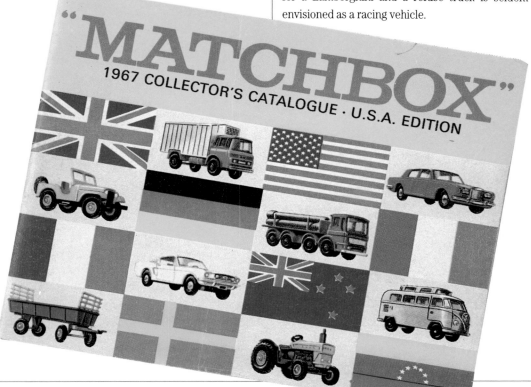

"MATCHBOX"
1967 COLLECTOR'S CATALOGUE · U.S.A. EDITION

CATALOGUE COVERS

Catalogue covers depict changes in terminology, if not in emphasis, over the years. From 1960 to 1963, they carried the phrase, "All the Matchbox pocket-money toys by Lesney" or simply, "Matchbox Series International Pocket Catalogue, Pocket-money toys by Lesney". But in 1964, the pocket-money phrase was dropped and in its place was the label, "Matchbox Collector's Catalogue". In 1976–82, the booklet was called the "Matchbox Catalogue". In 1982–83, there was a brief return to "Collector's Catalogue" before the appearance of the special 1983 edition carrying the first of the ultra-brief titles – simply "Matchbox 1983" – the style that has continued until the present.

Catalogue covers, both front and back, hint at Matchbox marketing, too. Beginning in 1962, catalogues were printed in other languages for countries where Matchbox had markets or hoped to develop them. These pocket-sized booklets, therefore, appeared fairly steadily in French, German, Italian, Spanish, Dutch and Japanese and, sporadically, in still other languages. International catalogues sometimes contained charts of selling prices in the various countries where they were to be circulated.

Naturally, these catalogues were some buyers' first introductions to the company's new lines. They were like an open line through to the thinking of company officials at the time.

Convoys were introduced in 1983 with the words, "Let them Truckers roll! Join our latest convoy of Peterbilts and Kenworths and play King of the Road with these brand new miniature models of giant, long-haul trucks".

Sea Kings, the series of ships that might as well have been torpedoed because they went down so quickly, was introduced thus: "Matchbox brings you an exciting new range of models, Sea Kings. Super-detailed fighting ships, finished in superb colour and armed for action. All the models have Superfast wheels for fast manoeuvres."

▼ BOTTOM LEFT

The 1963 edition of the Matchbox Series International Pocket Catalogue still contained the phrase "Pocket-money Toys by Lesney" – a phrase that was scrapped the following year. The cover featured the new No 53 Mercedes 220 SE coupé with a Matchbox first – opening doors.

▼ BOTTOM CENTRE

Catalogue terminology took a new turn in 1964 when the phrase "Pocket-money Toys by Lesney" was dropped and the catalogue was called a "Collector's" catalogue.

▼ BOTTOM RIGHT

There were several versions of the 1982/83 catalogue (actually intended to cover the 1982 market) including the Dutch (top), US and German editions. All gave front-billing to Convoys introduced that year. The announcement of the Code Red series of vehicles, coinciding with the television show, was also pictured in this catalogue.

1983 CATALOGUE

The slim, very limited 1983 catalogue, is a stark contrast to the high-wheeling early days, and particularly to the 1970 catalogue which was so filled with innovative vehicles and accessories.

Inside the front cover, the 1983 noted: "This year we're celebrating 30 years of toy making by bringing you the very best in tough, action-packed models that look like the real thing. There's a terrific choice including exciting, brand new models, and lots of your old favourites".

But the celebration year catalogue could be compared to a birthday cake with just one candle for every decade. Just four major lines (1–75, Convoy, Models of Yesteryear and SuperKings) were represented. Other catalogues, both before and after this number, have shown a much broader range of Matchbox products.

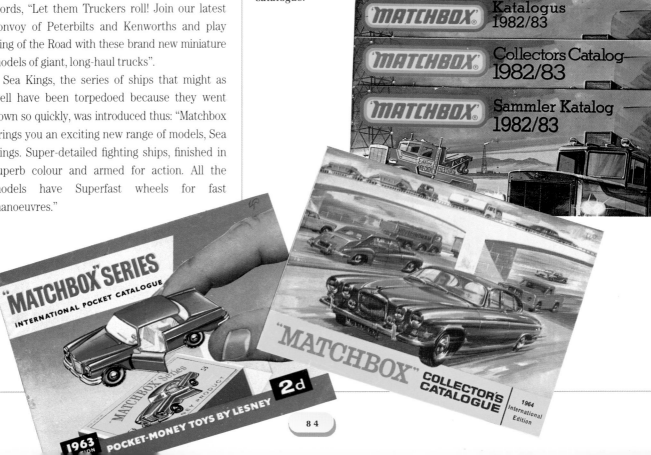

focus on catalogues. They prefer the less-crowded conditions and the open road this line of Matchbox products afford compared with the bumper-to-bumper, highly competitive collecting of diecast categories, like Models of Yesteryear. While others seek early Lesney toys or Superkings, they are on the lookout for the early Lesney fold-out leaflets of 1957 and 1958, as well as the full run of standard catalogues (those with stapled pages).

But that is by no means where the quest ends. Specialized catalogues like those produced by the Germans or Australians for the Models of Yesteryear are sought after. The 1976 specialized catalogue of souvenirs (everything from cigar boxes to pen stands) is desirable.

It does not matter for which country the Matchbox catalogue was destined or whether the collector could read the language in which it was printed in, it still can be desirable. Naturally, the early catalogues (1958 onwards) and the fold-out sheets (beginning in 1957) that were their forerunners, are of particular interest.

But collecting some of the older catalogues, produced for the European market, can be a particular challenge as not many were kept. Lt Col James Smith (USA, retired) collects and deals in Matchbox catalogues and has produced a 68-page listing of all catalogues, their differences and the languages in which they have been printed. He explains his obsession: "Not having a particular catalogue becomes just as annoying as looking at an empty spot in a stamp album. Filling that space becomes essential."

Mint, or better-than-mint condition, catalogues command the best prices. To be mint, the booklet should be free of wrinkles, tears, stains or inside markings. They can show a little wear from being touched or passed around a few times. Pristine catalogues are mint-plus. They are the ones that never reached collectors' hands, found stored in boxes from the printer.

Like the diecast cars, catalogues plummet in value when they are marred by even minute scratches or marks, dog-eared pages or outlines of old coffee stains. Ironically, the avid collector who followed Matchbox advice to "tick off" the models he purchased in pencil, was ruining the value of his catalogue as a collector's item. According to Smith, the only extraneous writing permitted is the stamped or written name of a toy shop on a catalogue's back cover.

Collecting catalogues from the 1960s, 1970s and 1980s remains affordable, but all that could change if people wake up to what they are missing in these little booklets.

▲ **ABOVE**
Front covers of all 1971 catalogues presented the Scorpions which were electronically controlled and carried a telltale logo. Speed was the message for the 1973 catalogue with a Team Matchbox racing car on the front cover. The team's progress and wins on the racing circuit were then noted in the 1974 catalogue.

COLLECTING CATALOGUES

Because the catalogues are so much more than mere pages of cars and trucks and other lines of Matchbox products, it's no surprise that these little booklets have themselves become collector's items.

Full sets of catalogues are certainly not found in every collector's home. Indeed, some Matchbox fans are content to buy just one or two for reference. They want to get a feel for what the catalogues contained, or they want to compare the content with some specific items in their collections. Insatiable Matchbox collectors, those who have to have one of every product Matchbox has ever made, search for pocket and dealers' catalogues of every sort. Then there are those specialists who simply

An early accessory pack intended for use with Matchbox cars contained a simple set of eight road hazard signs in diecast metal. Missing from this line-up (crossroads, level crossing, farm animals, sharp curves, roundabout, school) are a sign for a bend in the road and another warning of a hospital zone.

E arly Matchbox vehicles were humble toys that didn't cost much and were intended for play in sand pits and backyards. But, before long, these unsalubrious destinations were seen as beneath these stylish cars and heavy duty trucks rolling off the assembly line. So, creative minds within the company set out to capture the imagination of children in the 1960s and 1970s and they did. They began by designing accessories, like the pack containing three Esso petrol pumps, a service station attendant and a tall Esso sign that could be spotted in the distance by young "drivers" whose petrol gauges were nearing "empty".

There also was a set of road signs indicating hazards like a double bend in the road, the terrifying British traffic circle called a "roundabout", and a train or level crossing.

Soon, there were roadways to go along with the road signs and petrol stations to go along with the petrol pumps. And that was only the beginning of the Matchbox efforts to make the company's toys ever-more interesting and exciting.

The long-time British Matchbox collector Ray Bush commented, "In my generation, children played with diecast push-along toy cars from ages five to fourteen. Nowadays, the age group for such play things is three to six because there are so many other attractions for those who are seven and older".

Another early accessory was a box-like plastic village store unit. The white building contained the information "Matchbox Shop Accessory Pack made in England by Lesney". Its windows were filled with foods from cornflakes and cheese to eggs and butter.

ROADWAYS

Roadways were the most obvious accessories for the cars and, through the years, Matchbox designers introduced all kinds of variations that went far beyond the simple, basic cardboard road mats that were first produced for travelling by Matchbox.

Along with the basic roadway came additional sets like: "Heart of London", picturing tourist attractions, Big Ben and Tower Bridge, Piccadilly Circus, and well-known streets like Regent Street and Haymarket; "Queen's London" with Buckingham Palace, St James' Park and Admiralty Arch; and a race track setting, complete with pits and grandstands. Additional sets in this basic cardboard roadway series included the R-2 construction site (described in the 1968 catalogue as "A realistically coloured construction site with three-dimensional stand-up buildings and all that construction sites contain", and the R-3 Farmyard which was designed for all the tractors, trailers and combine harvesters a young Matchbox customer could purchase.

After these "fold away" playgrounds, came the impressive Matchbox "Build-A-Road", marketed in the United States in the late 1960s. The 1968 pocket catalogue announced this more creative approach to road building, telling Matchbox enthusiasts who may have had their early creativity "stifled" by the printed cardboard roads, "Now you can design and build your very own roadway, scaled just right for Matchbox Models". The Super Build-A-Road, with more than 90 pieces and at least seven different possibilities for roadway designs, sold for $7.

The G-4 Grand Prix Set labelled "A Lesney Product" contained vehicles numbered 13, 14, 19, 32, 41, 47, 52 and 73. The line-up included a roadway, racing cars, a tow-away truck for the vehicles that were destroyed and an ambulance to transport injured racing car drivers.

Early attempts by Matchbox to create play settings for cars and trucks were very simple. This R-3 in the roadway series consisted of a flat mat and a foldaway cardboard farm but, even so, it represented an advance on earlier, simple, flat cardboard mats.

The G-1 Motorway set included everything a child needed for a good time – assorted vehicles from the 1–75 series as well as a cardboard roadway and a set of road signs.

The G-8 Construction Set included five Matchbox King Size vehicles and was issued in 1964. Vehicles were the K-1 8-wheel tipper truck; K-7 rear dumper; K-10 tractor shovel; K-13 concrete truck and K-14 jumbo crane.

Matchbox Build-A-Road was a far more sophisticated kit than earlier cardboard roadways. These sets, scaled specially for Matchbox models, were made by snapping together plastic pieces to create a wide variety of roadway patterns.

The Matchbox Motorway included speed controllers and an electric power pack, as well as adapters so that any Matchbox model could be used on this track.

Still another option for Matchbox "drivers" was the Matchbox Motorway that cost a hefty $22.95 in 1969 but, as the catalogue promised, would "put action in your Matchbox Collection". With special adapters to fit any Matchbox model, variable speed controllers and an electric power pack, cars could race around the track without any hands having to touch them.

The switch to Superfast wheels ushered in a new era for roadways. Staid construction sites, farmyards and motorways faded quickly and were replaced by dramatic Superfast Tracks with all kinds of accessories designed to add to the thrills of Matchbox "driving". There were, for example, the SF-1 Speed Set (a basic drag strip), the SF-2 Loop Set (which took the car in an airborne circle), and the SF-3 Curve and Space Leap Set (after coming around a curve, a car would fly over an open space before landing on more track). The lights at Matchbox must have burned late to come up with these roadways to win back those buyers switching to Hot Wheels.

▼ BELOW

Matchbox Super Garage was introduced in the 1979/80 pocket catalogue as a new three-level garage that had an operating parking lift, moveable auto ramps and a rotating Matchbox Garage sign as well as a full-colour playmat.

▼ BELOW

This "Showroom and Service Station for Matchbox Toys" was produced at the end of the 1950s. It first came out with a yellow building and red base, but later was released with a red building and yellow base. Petrol pumps had to be purchased separately to make this a "working" station.

► OPPOSITE TOP

The Matchbox City Garage and the Super Spin Car Wash were additional accessories that enabled children to duplicate some of the driving their parents did. They could pull into the city garage, with its 25 parking spaces, spring-loaded car lift, drive down the ramp to pay for their ticket and take a spin around the playmat before heading for the Super Spin Car Wash.

► OPPOSITE BOTTOM

The Matchbox Autopark set, dated 1970, was billed as "The Skypark of the Future". It contained an "autopark", a forecourt, one curved track and a set of sheltered petrol pumps. Cars and batteries to operate the ferris-wheel style parking system were not included.

SERVICE STATIONS, FIRE STATIONS AND GARAGES

Early service stations, both one and two storeys high, as well as a fire station, captured the imagination of those who wanted their roads to have some specific destination. Although there were variations, the earliest version of a service station was one-storey and inner-city sized. Coloured red and yellow, it was quite compact.

In contrast, the BP petrol station pictured in the 1966 pocket catalogue was expansive, the kind of sprawling suburban structure that's expected where there's room to spread out. It had showrooms on two floors and a forecourt for petrol pumps. There was also a service ramp-incline from the ground to the first floor level. Along with the BP logo, "Matchbox Sales & Service Station" was printed along the roofline.

Fire stations, with shiny red engines, sirens and bells, have long appealed to children who dream of racing from the station to put out fires. The Matchbox fire station featured side-by-side double doors in the engine house and a firemen's pole from the second to the ground floor. It, like the service station, cost $3 in 1966 and came fully assembled.

Garages have come in all shapes and sizes progressing far beyond the early combination petrol stations and garages. Matchbox Autopark, with a 1970 copyright on the box, was billed as "The Sky Park of the Future". Battery operated, it looked something like an enclosed Ferris wheel for cars and rotated to allow young "attendants" to park their cars.

The 1972 pocket catalogue featured Matchbox Station Maker which contained all the parts a youngster needed to build a garage to his own shape and size. It could be on one level or a multi-storey.

On the other hand, in the towering three-level Matchbox Super Garage pictured in the 1979/80 and 1981/82 pocket catalogues the features were fixed. On the first floor there were car-care, spare parts and service centres and in the rest of the structure an operating parking lift, moveable auto ramps and a rotating Matchbox Garage sign.

Since then, there have been many more freestanding play environments and structures produced by Matchbox including construction yards, container ports, lorry parks and even a car wash. All these structures could be called the forerunners to Play Track combinations of roads and buildings, introduced in the early 1980s, and the Motor City sets of the late 1980s and early 1990s.

EPHEMERA

Those who like to acquire more ephemeral goods relating to the company can search out Matchbox calendars, which were first printed in the 1980s. They can look for an early sixties series of hard-to-find books for painting or colouring. These "life-savers" were designed to keep children amused when they had to be indoors rather than playing outside with the diecast miniatures.

Matchbox picture puzzles, advertised in the 1969 pocket catalogue, featured diecast models in life-like settings such as a tractor in a field or buses on a mountain roadway. These full-colour jigsaws could be assembled to create "beautiful pictures to hang on your wall". Frames were to have the model introduction date and description plaque printed on them.

There was even a Matchbox story book called *Mike and the Model Makers*, a children's version of how Matchbox models were made. It began with Mike's description, "There was a building so long I could not see the other end. Up on the roof there was a sign. It was a name I didn't know. And in the street, a strange coloured bus for London – blue – then suddenly, another bus came by and I saw on the side of it – 'Matchbox'. Lesney means 'Matchbox'! Now I knew what Daddy meant when he was talking about the greatest automobile factory in the world."

According to the 1970 pocket catalogue, this little book with full colour drawings, was "a must for all

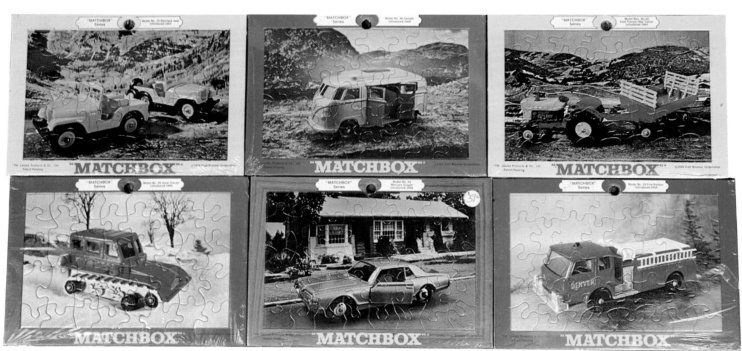

▲ OPPOSITE

"Matchbox Keeps on Trucking", was a giant-sized colouring book produced in 1988 by Stoneway Books Ltd of Southeastern Pennsylvania.

◄ OPPOSITE BOTTOM

Matchbox picture puzzles, each measuring 5 by 7 inches, were advertised in the 1969 collector's catalogue and were priced at 39 cents in the United States. Specially designed with self-adhesive backing, they could be permanently mounted to hang as a picture or they could be used as a puzzle. Left to right, on the top, they are the No 72

▲ ABOVE

This tinplate sign was produced in America in 1968, obtained by an Australian collector who sold it to a German dealer, who in turn sold it to the Chester Toy Museum.

Standard Jeep, introduced in 1967; the No 34 Camper, introduced in 1968; the No 39 and No 40 Ford tractor and hay trailer introduced in 1967. On the bottom are: No 35 Snow tractor introduced in 1965; No 62 Mercury Cougar introduced in 1968 and the No 29 fire pumper introduced in 1969. All were marked "1969, Fred Bronner Corp".

▲ ABOVE

GAF View-Master Grand Prix was a racing game for 2 to 4 people and included two dice, four coloured flags and four Matchbox racers.

◄ LEFT

Still another example of Matchbox success in jigsaw fashion. This time, when assembled, the puzzle resembled a colourful car park with some tame and some wild vehicles.

"MATCHBOX" traffic game

INCLUDES TWO "MATCHBOX" CARS

- LIVELY ACTION WITH THE ROTATING TRAFFIC SIGNAL
- CHOICE AND CHANCE...PLAYS DIFFERENTLY EVERY TIME
- FUN FOR 2 TO 4 PLAYERS AGES 8 TO 14
- EXCITING GAME FOR

COLLECTORS

▲ **ABOVE**

The Matchbox Traffic Game, billed as an "exciting game for Matchbox collectors", was for 2 to 4 players ages 8–14. It included two Matchbox cars as well as "lively action with a rotating traffic signal that indicated different plays".

Matchbox collectors and suitable for children of all ages."

Board games, incorporating the diecast vehicles, will appeal to Matchbox enthusiasts as well as more generalized collectors. The Matchbox Traffic Game, for two or four players, included two Matchbox cars, mileage measurer, chance cards, game board, traffic signal and instructions. The Matchbox Crash Game, new in 1970, came with four diecast miniatures. "Watch your car soar to the front with the throw of a dice – change lanes and outwit your rivals but be careful of the crash area – you can lose your lead", the copy ran.

Those who played with other Matchbox toys might remember the Magnet Action Centres and the Steer-N-Go toys. The Magnet Action Centres had tiny magnet-operated people who moved to load and service Matchbox models. There were three different versions, the Magnetic Action Repair Centre, the Magnetic Action Freight Centre and the Magnetic Action Farm Centre.

Steer-N-Go put young Matchbox fans in the driver's seat long before they could be licensed to drive on real roads. The toy, which included a simulated wood steering wheel, gear lever, ignition switch, hand brake, lap counter and timing device, featured a rotating disc that presented the driving challenges similar to those on a real country road.

Advised the toy-filled 1970 catalogue, "Slip into first gear, you are in motion. Looks easy? Wait until you change into second and try to take that sharp right hand turn. Better change into third gear – now you are really travelling but watch out, time is running out. There will be many spills and thrills before you master the roadway."

For those accustomed to the constant stream of new issues in the diecast lines, it probably came as no surprise that there were three additional driving courses to go with the Steer-N-Go game: the village roadway with six buildings; the dune buggy roadway with marking flags charting a driving course on the sand and a Grand Prix roadway, with a grandstand and finishing gate.

No. 5501

▼ BELOW

This fire station set was something of a cross-cultural product because the fire station was British as were the ambulance and fire engines (one is missing from the picture) but an American fire chief's vehicle also was included.

▲ ABOVE

The Motor City Municipal Parking Set included more than 70 pieces and like earlier Build-A-Road sets, enabled the young builder to construct a parking system of his own design. The complete playset included traffic lights, signs, street lights, petrol pumps and a working vehicle lift. It could be constructed horizontally or vertically or, as the advertising copy said, "any way you can imagine".

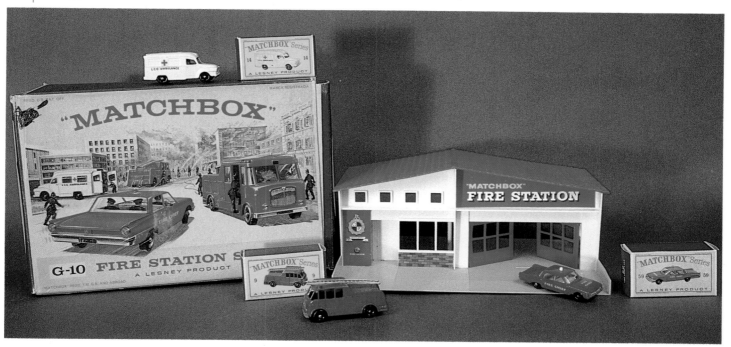

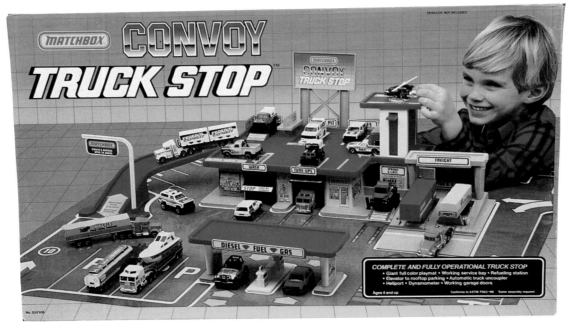

◄ LEFT

This preproduction box for a Matchbox Sounds of Service Repair Centre was advertised in the 1982/83 collectors' catalogue as a "total play environment with the sophistication of a large, modern service centre". It included an operating elevator, two lifts, a grease pit, two service bays, a dynamometer, exit ramp, two parking levels and a 20 by 30-in (50 by 75-cm) playmat. The exclusive feature, thanks to electronics, was accompanying car sounds , such as an engine starting.

◄ LEFT

The creation of the Convoys also created a "need" for a new play set – a Matchbox Convoy Truck Stop. After all, where were young "truckers" going to be able to stop for food and fuel when "driving" their 18 wheelers? This Convoy Truck Stop had many of the same characteristics as other playsets including the rooftop lift, heliport, dynamometer and playmat. It also had a working service bay and garage doors, as well as an automatic truck uncoupler and a refueling centre for both diesel and petrol.

◄ LEFT

Another view of the Super Spin Car Wash with a lineup of "customers" waiting to give it a try. According to Matchbox writers, "Half the fun of owning a car is keeping it clean." This unit actually showered cars with water as they moved along a conveyor belt and then spun them dry!

COLLECTORS' CASES

But there was still another problem area for those who played with Matchbox vehicles, roadways and buildings which could be solved by more products. That is, customers needed "garages" for their cars and lorries when they had finished playing with them.

Matchbox collectors' cases addressed the need, encouraging children to organize and store their diecast vehicles neatly.

At first, these collectors' cases were basic, utilitarian "boxes", but in the years that followed, Matchbox designers came up with some imaginative storage containers. In 1968 there were two cases, one for 48 models and another one for 18 of scuff-resistant washable vinyl with nickel-plated snap locks and strong plastic handles. A year later, there were 72- and 24-model cases that had plastic, lift-out trays.

There's no doubt, however, that buyers of these early cases would have envied later carrying-case designs that stored the models in containers shaped like a tool box, a convoy truck, a city garage, a racing car and a steering wheel.

▲ **ABOVE**

The Rescue Center Play Hat makes the transition between play area and carrying case because it is both. Closed, it took the shape of a bright red hard hat. Open, it was the location for police and fire headquarters, a medical centre and a rescue helicopter landing pad. Although many vehicles were shown with it, there was just one free rescue vehicle included with the set.

▼ **BELOW**

Matchbox Official Collectors Carrying Cases have been produced as ordinary rectangular suitcase designs, but other more fantastic containers have been conceived by Matchbox designers for the "parking and storage" of vehicles.

▶ **RIGHT**

Designers were going for gold when they came up with this 48-car carrying case shaped like a racing car. The handle is on the rocker panel between the two wheels.

▼ **BELOW**

Although the 1970 pocket catalogue shows ordinary collectors' cases with the label "Superfast Collectors' Cases", a special unit was produced during 1970. Marked "1970 Matchbox, Lesney Products & Co. Ltd, London, England", this case had extra room beyond that needed to store the 1–75 line-up.

▶ **RIGHT**

Convoys not only inspired Matchbox designers to develop a truck stop play set but also stimulated them to produce a new carrying case decorated to look like a truck. Two versions were available – one that held 36 Matchbox models and a larger one with a 48-car capacity.

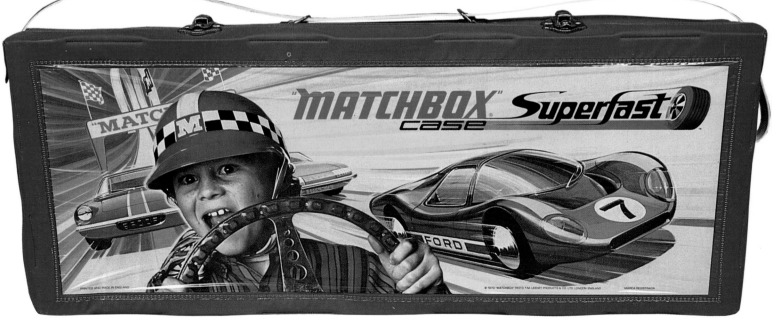

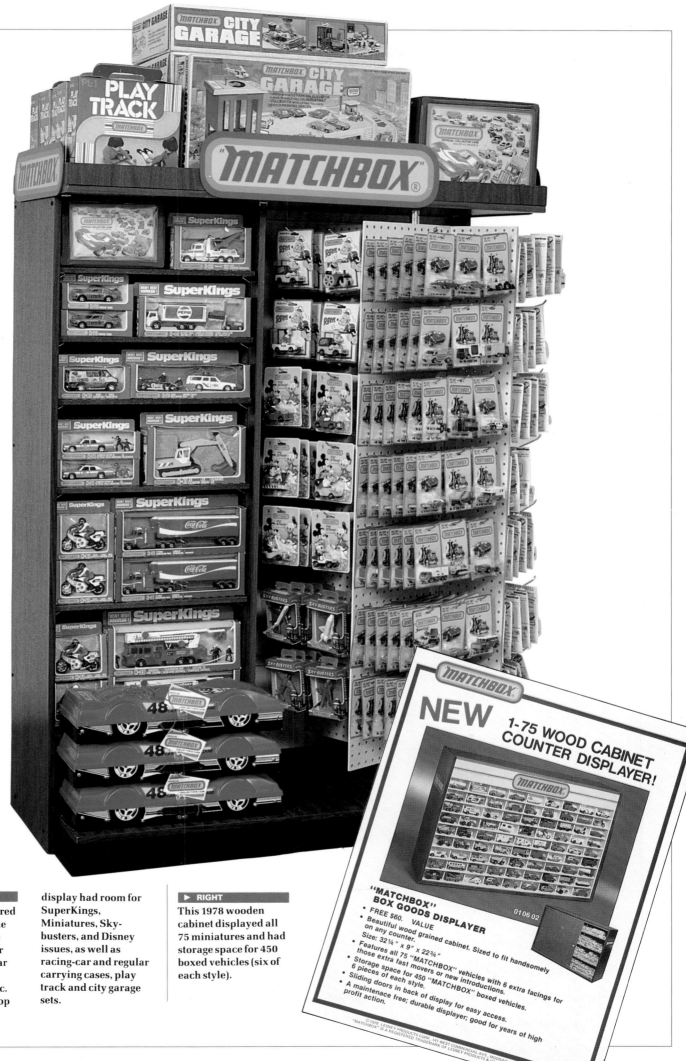

▲ ABOVE

Matchbox had covered many miles since the days of simple shop displays for 1-75s or Models of Yesteryear made of wood, cardboard or plastic. This early 1980s shop display had room for SuperKings, Miniatures, Sky-busters, and Disney issues, as well as racing-car and regular carrying cases, play track and city garage sets.

▶ RIGHT

This 1978 wooden cabinet displayed all 75 miniatures and had storage space for 450 boxed vehicles (six of each style).

NEW 1-75 WOOD CABINET COUNTER DISPLAYER!

"MATCHBOX" BOX GOODS DISPLAYER

0106 02

- FREE $60. VALUE
- Beautiful wood grained cabinet. Sized to fit handsomely on any counter.
  Size: 32¼" x 9" x 22¾"
- Features all 75 "MATCHBOX" vehicles with 6 extra facings for those extra fast movers or new introductions.
- Storage space for 450 "MATCHBOX" boxed vehicles. 6 pieces of each style.
- Sliding doors in back of display for easy access.
- A maintenance free; durable displayer; good for years of high profit action.

BEYOND THE BASICS

Over the years, Matchbox product lines have diversified in about as many directions as vehicles going to and from Hackney Wick (where the company headquarters were located). There have been dolls, plastic models, miniature pub signs, miniature dogs, and hand-held plastic puzzles, to say nothing of souvenir paperweights featuring such London landmarks as St Paul's and Big Ben. But there are other lines that are of more interest to those who love the diecast vehicles.

For those with lots of space, old dealer display cases can be found in cardboard, wood and plastic. They can be filled with vehicles just as they used to be in toy shops everywhere.

Lesney Veteran Car Gifts, produced in the late 1960s and well into the 1970s, marketed the Models of Yesteryear in a new way – with silver and gold finishes and usually mounted on various kinds of giftware. A double pen stand had a 1907 Rolls-Royce Silver Ghost mounted between the two pens. A large wooden cigarette box came with a 1911 Model T Ford or a 1928 Mercedes Benz on its lid. Ash trays in the 1967 catalogue were available with any one of six Models of Yesteryear while pipe smokers had to be satisfied with a choice of two vehicles on their pipe trays.

Before the giftware line came to an end, diecast vehicles (as well as a few aeroplanes and pistols) would be used on everything from bookends and desk calendars to thermometers and pipe racks. Some of the plated vehicles were sold separately, too, in wooden display cases for collectors.

▼ **BOTTOM**
A line of Matchbox souvenirs included this ashtray that measured 7⅝ by 5⅜ in (19 by 13.5 cm) and was decorated with a 1934 Riley with silver body and red fenders.

▼ **BELOW**
This plated model of a Spitfire has proved to be a very collectable if "non-earthbound" vehicle, made during the 1970s.

▲ ABOVE

Matchbox in Germany designed this clever combination of a clock and display stand in 1991. It proved to be too expensive, however, to be of use to the other markets and was not exported.

◀ LEFT

This is one of the very first colouring books produced by Lesney over 30 years ago. It is not known how many of these survived uncoloured.

Museums

MATCHBOX ROAD

Enough vehicles to cause the world's largest traffic jam have come to a halt where Everett Marshall III stands in Newfield, NJ. But there's no sound of honking horns or drivers' exploding tempers in this peaceful, crossroads town. Meanwhile, Charlie Mack manages to park more than 14,000 vehicles in a space no larger than a residential home – his own. Both men started as ordinary Matchbox collectors and now have established American museums devoted to Matchbox toys. There are few additional public collections of this magnitude other than the Matchbox Room in the Chester Toy Museum in England and the Little Wheels Exhibit in the Power House Museum in Australia.

Everett Marshall's New Jersey museum, Matchbox Road, first opened in November 1991 in a renovated three-car garage. About a year later, he held a grand reopening after doubling the museum's size and adding a collectors' shop.

Marshall, who played with Matchbox toys as a child, didn't purchase more of the models until 1980 when he heard rumours that Matchbox was going to go bankrupt. He decided to buy each of that year's 1–75 line and save them for his son who was then two years old. He stopped at a large toy store and began selecting cars and trucks. "As I was picking the vehicles, I started seeing colour variations between what were supposedly the same vehicles. I never realized there were so many differences and bought one of every different model and variation the store had."

He started buying still more variations, by making weekly trips to toy shops and attending toy shows. About the time he realized he was "hooked" on the Matchbox habit, he also joined the club Matchbox USA. Marshall began planning a museum in 1985, when his collection outgrew his basement.

Today, his museum, which is open by appointment, is well-known for its collection of Superfast models, SuperKing models, Convoys, Major Packs, and 1–75 Regular Wheels as well as the White Rose releases and MB38s. Tucked in nooks and crannies are additional vehicles including

Dinky and some of the ill-fated Sea Kings. He has not concentrated on Models of Yesteryear or early Lesney toys and, although Marshall has stopped collecting Lledo vehicles (made in the UK by former Matchbox founder Jack Odell), he maintains most of his collection in a nearby building.

Marshall also has amassed a representative assortment of other associated items, including early cardboard roadways, garages, racing tracks, jigsaw puzzles and collectors' carrying cases.

◄ LEFT
Everett Marshall, founder of Matchbox Road (one of two American Museums devoted to Matchbox), expanded his display areas and reopened the museum in Newfield, NJ, in 1992.

MATCHBOX & LESNEY TOY MUSEUM

Charlie Mack, who founded the club Matchbox USA and edits the club's monthly publication Matchbox USA, opened his Matchbox & Lesney Toy Museum in September 1992 in four rooms of his basement as well as two additional rooms in his Durham, Connecticut home.

Mack, an admitted "Matchbox-aholic", presents a much more diverse collection than Matchbox Road. His museum is also only open by appointment. "I have one of every diecast piece Matchbox made from 1947, although I don't have all the colour variations", he says. In addition to his excellent collection of early Lesney toys, he also has a strong collection of resin prototype and preproduction

▼ BELOW
This MB38 van, in robin's egg blue with darker blue roof and fenders, advertises the Toy Museum at Chester, England which contains a collection of Matchbox toys. The van measures 3 inches long and its rear doors say: "For Kids of All Ages, 42 Bridge St. Rows, Chester, England, Tel. 0244-316251". The base reads, "Matchbox International, 1979. Made in Macau".

models for vehicles in the 1–75, Models of Yesteryear, Convoy and Skybuster lines.

But his collection goes well beyond diecast vehicles and includes play sets, catalogues and literature and what Mack calls "weird and crazy stuff", like dolls, stuffed animals, Pee Wee Herman items, licensed toys, Code 3s (a normal Matchbox model, changed by colour, design or decoration, without the knowledge or approval of Matchbox), as well as an extensive display of on-pack offers which matches the product with the vehicle buyers received, if they followed all the directions printed on a box or can.

According to Mack, the new museum contains a range of Matchbox products from the common (still in the $1 range) to the very rare items that are priced in the thousands.

CHESTER TOY MUSEUM

England's Chester Toy Museum (13A Lower Bridge Street Row, Chester, UK), features an extensive collection of Models of Yesteryear models as well as some of the rarest of Matchbox models in its Matchbox Room.

POWER HOUSE MUSEUM

Peter Cox, curator of the Power House Museum, 500 Harris St, Sydney, Australia, said his museum's collection includes the 1–75 series of miniatures, an extensive collection of Models of Yesteryear, as well as Major Pack and Kingsize models, Sea Kings, Skybusters, Battle Kings, and Convoys, in addition to gift sets, souvenirs, roadways, boxed sets, collectors' catalogues and some rare special issues.

In 1985 the Power House Museum was given its Matchbox Toy collection by Matchbox Toys Pty Ltd and the organization has continued to keep the collection up-to-date with regular donations of the latest releases.

Lledo

▶ **ABOVE**
This version of the
DG15 bus advertised
"Take Hall's Wine and
Defy Influenza". The
silver roofed double-
decker bus measured
3¼ in (8 cm) long.

n 1982, seven years after Jack Odell resigned from Lesney Products, the Midland Bank asked him to return to Lesney to see what he could do to save the firm which was facing imminent bankruptcy. Lesney owed £26 million, which by today's standards was a relatively small sum. As Odell observed, taking over Lesney at this time was like being asked to assume command of the *Titanic* ten minutes before she sank. He would be able to do very little before the receivers were called in.

When the receivers took over, virtually all production stopped, idling nearly all of Lesney's workers because at the time it was not certain whether Lesney's would be bought and by which firm it might be acquired. Jack Odell particularly worried about the toolroom personnel and tried to think of ways he could alleviate their plight.

The idea finally came to him when the new owners, Universal, decided to move all Matchbox production out of the UK, which meant the permanent idling of many UK factories filled with machines designed, for the most part, by Odell himself. Odell decided to create a line of diecast toys, larger than the miniature Matchbox series and yet not quite as large as his Yesteryears brainchild. The result was Lledo. The name of the company was a throwback to his code name during his army years – his name spelled backwards.

The first six Lledo models were created in the development toolrooms at Lesney. Odell chose what he considered to be the best ten of Lesney's old personnel to be the core of his design and production staff. Even today, most of the machine operators at Lledo are ex-Lesney employees, making all the components of Lledo models on equipment that was originally Lesney-owned before the bankruptcy in 1982.

Odell then went in search of a place to manufacture his models, and found a suitable building at a former gas works next to the Ponders End railway station near Enfield in North London (within a stone's throw of the Lesney factory at Enfield).

To obtain the other necessary personnel for his venture, he had letters pushed through the letter boxes of all three high-rise buildings nearby, housing mostly new immigrants. Within a short time, Odell had all the labour he needed for his new company.

The first six Lledo models were released at Easter 1983 and numbered 001–006. They included a Tram (DG001), a Milk Float (DG002), a Delivery Van (DG003), an Omnibus (DG004) and a Fire Engine (DG005). The final model issued, and the biggest success of the six, was a Ford Model T Van (DG006), and it was a particularly charming one.

Five of these first six models were less than overwhelming successes. Always having a soft spot for horse-drawn vehicles, Odell created the first Lledo production with a disproportionate number. Lledo's founder thought that the horse-drawn vehicles might appeal more to women collectors but, ultimately, Odell had to admit that the mechanically-powered vehicles sold much better and the horse-drawn ones were dropped from the line. Ever since, with two exceptions, all Lledo models have been of mechanically powered vehicles.

▼ BELOW
The fifth vehicle in the line was the DG5 – a horse-drawn fire engine pulled by two black horses and manned by three blue plastic firemen (who were loose and could topple off when the engine was racing to a fire). The engine was marked "Doorn 60".

The "Downtown 3" tram was the first of several horse-drawn vehicles produced shortly after Jack Odell founded Lledo. There were five rows of seats in the tram that was pulled by one black horse. It measured 4¾ in (11.9 cm) long and was marked on the bottom with "Days Gone/DG1/ Made in England by Lledo".

About this time, the first promotional issues were created, opening up a market that would prove both boon and bane to collectors. The Model T Ford Van, in the style of the Models of Yesteryear, became the basis for the promotional models because of the useful area on the sides on which tampo and labels could be placed. To keep going, Odell accepted orders for very short run models in different colours and with different logos. Had it not been for these promotional models, Lledo might have followed Lesney to bankruptcy even though Lledo's production was a fraction of what Lesney's had been during its heyday when fifteen factories were kept humming with Matchbox production.

The creation of the promotional models produced something of a problem for Odell in that some way needed to be found to identify the two different lines, which even shared the same castings. There had been confusion created when Matchbox had not kept promotional models separate from the regular line. Ray Bush argued emphatically that the regular issue models and the promotional ones should be kept as separate ranges. Ultimately, the

undersides of the cars were marked either "Days Gone" or "Promotional Model".

Questions about the promotional model range do arise from time to time because the earliest production samples did not possess the identifying insert on their undersides, but most knowledgeable collectors now know those models that were really early promotional models but issued within the Days Gone line. A bigger problem are those Code 3 models that were originally Days Gone samples that have been changed without Lledo approval by unauthorized third parties. (Lledo models also utilize the coding system used for the Matchbox lines.)

Because of the small scale of the venture, Lledo wanted to avoid involvement in warehousing and sales. Just as in the early Lesney days when Moko carried out the marketing operations for Lesney, Odell used a separate marketing company to handle the distribution of Lledo – the Saltern Agency, operated by Andrew Smith, the son of Leslie Smith. Andrew Smith was soon joined by an ex-Lesney employee Ron Ping. However, problems developed

A Lledo Model T Ford Van served as a View Van for Big Ben. It measured 2¾ in (6.8 cm) long and was labelled with: "Lledo promotional model" and "Made in England". Lledo finished the basic paint jobs on the vans, but for the View Van lines, sold them to others who added the postcard-style scenes and sold them at various tourist attractions. The View Vans are considered Code 2s.

◀ LEFT

Another Lledo promotional model was this Model T Ford Tanker. This one was made for Everett Marshall of Marshall's Fuel Service in Newfield, NJ (Marshall is also the founder of the American museum called Matchbox Road).

▶ RIGHT

This DG23 bus was a silver Greyhound Scenicruiser with three roof-top viewing windows.

▼ BELOW
The Edocar series of vehicles were produced by Lledo for sales in the Netherlands. This Edocar Old Time Series is a 1926 Model T Ford Petrol Tanker. Edocar is the trademark of Fred Beheer BV.

EA - 1 1926 T-Ford Petrol Tanker

▲ ABOVE

Lledo Marathons were to feature more modern transportation vehicles and were intended also to be a bit larger in scale. Production began in 1987 and some five models were issued, with each repeated in a number of different liveries, but they did not sell well and so were discontinued. This Marathon Model for the Huddersfield Daily Examiner, advertised: "The Examiner delivers the news around here like no one else can".

and ultimately Lledo took over Saltern, including the warehousing space and the marketing of its models.

The year 1984 saw the issue of seven new Days Gone models: a Ford "Woody" Wagon (Estate) DG007; a Model T Ford Tanker, DG008; a Model A Ford Car (a touring car with no top), DG009; an Albion Single Decker Coach, DG010; a Large Horse-drawn Van, DG011, a Fire Engine, DG012; and a Model A Ford Van, DG013. The latter had a roof blade (a horizontal or diagonal raised advertising board) or a header (a vertical advertising board placed at the start of the roof).

Six new models greeted 1985: a Ford Model A Car (with top up), DG014; an AEC Double Deck Bus, DG015; a Heavy Goods Van, DG016; a Long Distance Coach, DG017; a Packard Van, DG018 (first released as an ambulance); and a Rolls-Royce Phantom II, DG019. With the introduction of the bus, Lledo discontinued the practice of including a set of plastic figures with each model.

Three more models followed in 1986. They were: the Model A Ford Stake Truck, DG020; a Chevrolet Van, DG021; and a Packard Town Van, DG022. Originally planned as a 1986 issue, the introduction of a Sceni-cruiser Bus, DG023, was postponed until early in 1987 because of production difficulties. Two Rolls-Royces – a Playboy Convertible Coupé, DG024 and a Silver Ghost Tourer, DG025 – were issued, along with a Chevrolet Bottle Truck, DG026, a Mack Breakdown Truck, DG027, and a Mack Canvas-Back Truck, DG028.

Today, the Days Gone range continues to expand. From 1987 to 1992, a further 22 models have been added to the series.

COLLECTING LLEDO

Any collector who decides to collect Lledo will have to make some decisions. First of all, the collector will need to decide what he wants to collect. Of course, the regular Days Gone series is available, and that range includes the basic models that again, like Matchbox, were issued in a variety of colours and liveries over their lifetime. Also, along with the regular Days Gone issues exists a confusing plethora of promotional models. Lledo has also issued special series of models for various companies, such as Hartoy (the previous US distributor of Lledo), Tesco supermarket chain in the UK, and the Edocar series introduced in the Netherlands. Lledo has also allowed some of its basic painted production to be altered with scenes from popular UK tourist attractions, thereby creating a number of Code 2 models. In 1987, Lledo issued a new series of models that created a line of modern transportation vehicles in a size slightly larger than the Days Gone line. Called Marathons, these five issues in various liveries were not good sellers and all work on this series has ceased.

What you decide to collect might be affected by availability. In the US, Lledo distribution is patchy at best. Some speciality collectors' shops do carry Lledo models. For the most part, a prospective collector will be greeted by puzzled looks if he asks for Lledo. Those vendors who carry the line do so by having some direct connection to stockists in the UK. And very few, if any, US outlets will carry all of the variations of the regular series or the promotional models. The American collector who decides that Lledo models are for him will definitely be crossing the Atlantic to gain access to the full range of his chosen speciality.

SPOTTING FAKES

Along with collecting the promotional model comes the problem of fakes. The logo of a regular Days Gone model is printed with tampo, but the promotional models also use labels and decals, which is one way for collectors to tell the promotional models from the regular series. However, the Code 3 models also use decals and transfers, and it is sometimes impossible to tell the Lledo-issued promotional models from the Code 3 ones. If a collector of promotional models is also collecting Code 3s, then the only problem will be determining into which part of his collection to place the model.

But if a collector is not collecting Code 3s, the stray one can be an expensive, unwelcome interloper.

Boxes can also be a problem, as Lledo has used a variety of packaging. Even some regular Days Gone models were issued in special boxes, such as some created for the London toy shop, Hamley's. Also, some were issued with certificates attesting to their uniqueness as promotional or commemorative models.

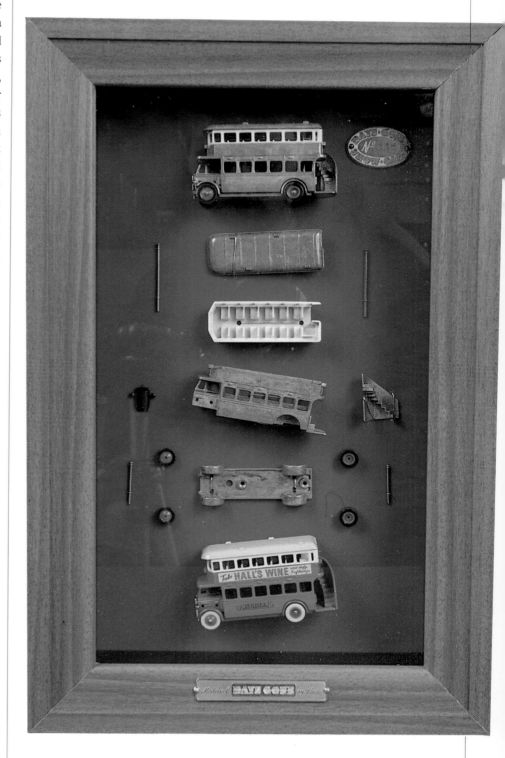

▼ BELOW
Limited Edition No 335 showed the bits and pieces used to create a version of the DG15 double-decker bus. The wooden presentation case measured 10½ by 16⅝ in (26 by 41.5 cm) and was produced before 1985.

Bibliography & Acknowledgements

Bowdidge, Philip, "*Matchbox®" Miniatures 1 to 75, 1953–1990* (Ashley, UK: Philip Bowdidge, 1990).

Bryant, Adam, "Making a Difference: Matchmaker for Matchbox®". *The New York Times*, 10 May 1992, Section B, p 8, col 5.

Bryant, Adam, "Company News: Tyco Toys Planning to Acquire Matchbox®", *The New York Times*, 7 May 1992, Section D, p 5, col 3.

Force, Dr Edward, *Matchbox® and Lledo™ Toys* (West Chester, Pa, USA: Schiffer Publishing, 1988).

Mack, Charles, *Lesney's Matchbox® Toys. Regular Wheel Years, 1947–1969* (West Chester, Pa, USA: Schiffer Publishing, 1992).

McGimpsey, Kevin and Stewart Orr *et al, Collecting Matchbox® Diecast Toys: The First Forty Years* (Chester, UK: Major Productions Limited, 1989).

Neuborne, Ellen and wire service reports, "Tyco stock rebounds from mid-June crash", *USA Today*, 1 July 1992, p 3B.

Rinker, Harry L, *Collector's Guide to Toys, Games & Puzzles* (Radnor, Pa, USA: Wallace-Homestead Book Company, 1991).

Smith, Lt Col James W, *Listing of Matchbox® Catalogues* (68 pages) (Norman, Ok, USA: James W Smith, June 1991).

Touby, Laurel, "Suddenly Tyco is Playing with the Big Kids", *Business Week*, 15 June 1992, pp 124, 126.

Thompson, Frank, *The Matchbox® Toy Price Guide 1953–1990*, Third Ed, (London: A & C Black, 1990).

Various Matchbox® Pocket Catalogues from 1963 to 1992.

We have many people to thank for keeping this Matchbox project on the road and heading in the right direction. They are:

Ray Bush, of Plymouth, England, whose knowledge of the early days of both Lesney Products and Lledo as well as personal friendships with Leslie Smith and Jack Odell were invaluable in writing a history of Matchbox.

Paul Carr, of Loughton, England, retired project leader of the Matchbox Research and Design Section, who shared his experiences and knowledge concerning the making and marketing of Matchbox toys, as well as information on the famous Matchbox MB38s.

Everett Marshall III, founder of the Matchbox Road Museum in Newfield, NJ, for allowing his collection to be photographed.

Ray Sytch of Amboy, NJ, who allowed his collection to be photographed.

Charles Mack, founder of both the Matchbox & Lesney Toy Museum in Durham, Ct and of the Matchbox USA Club, who traced the development of the collecting hobby as well as provided details on his new museum.

Lt Col James Smith, Norman, Ok, who knows Matchbox pocket catalogues from cover to cover.

Ron Slyder, founder of White Rose Collectibles of York, Pa, for information on White Rose and the collecting of Matchbox vehicles.

Craig Hill of Craig and Linda Hills' Collectors' Toys, Binghamton, NY.

Peter Cox, curator of the Power House Museum, Sydney, Australia.

Stewart Orr, of the Chester Toy Museum, England, for allowing access to the Matchbox Room for photography, and for contributing captions.

Mike Apnel, president of the Pennsylvania Matchbox Collectors' Club and owner of Kiddie Kar Kollectibles in Reading, Pa, as well as Pennsylvania Matchbox Collectors' Club members Bill Charles of Lancaster, Pa, and Linda Murray of Leola, Pa, for their guidance and resources in preparing this book.

Harry Rinker, Jr, and Ian Howes, whose photography for this book has made looking at Matchbox toys almost as enjoyable as those childhood days of playing with them.

Harry Rinker, Sr, who gave us the "push" that got us started on the project and provided guidance and advice all along the road.